Advanced Database®

---

with

Microsoft® Access

ICDL Professional®

Conor Jordan

Conor Jordan

This edition published 2022

Copyright © Conor Jordan 2022

E-mail: conorjordan@gmail.com

Web: www.digidiscover.com

ISBN: 978-1-7396547-4-0

The intent of this manual is to provide a guide for readers to help them understand the advanced word processing and the features associated with using Microsoft Access®.

Conor Jordan does not guarantee readers will pass their respective exams because of reading this book. Its purpose is to enable readers to better understand the applications that may or may not help them achieve their desired results in exams.

Revision sections are for practice purposes only and are not official ICDL tests. Sample tests for each module can be downloaded from the ICDL website to prepare students for their exams.

This book aims to give readers a clear understanding of the advanced features of Microsoft Access. It aims to achieve this by providing a step-by-step guide describing the skills needed to use this application effectively.

Downloading Resources

Resources associated with this book provide the opportunity to practice the techniques outlined. This will save the learner time to focus on the practical exercises. Visit www.digidiscover.com/downloads and click on the manual you are using.

Files should be saved in an ICDL Professional folder in 'Documents' on your computer.

Introduction

ICDL Professional is a series of digital skills modules developed to improve learners' employment prospects, capability, and competency and build on their existing knowledge. Subjects covered include advanced word processing, management spreadsheets, financial spreadsheets, advanced presentation, and advanced database. Learners can add to their learner profile using any combination of completed modules tailored to suit their workplace requirements.

The advanced modules, formally known as Advanced ECDL, which covered Microsoft Word, Excel, PowerPoint, and Access applications, have become part of the ICDL Professional series of computer modules. There are now fifteen separate modules, with a new e-commerce module soon becoming available.

The database guidance covered in this book may help readers develop their understanding of advanced Microsoft Access features and may prepare readers for their Advanced Database exam. Successful completion of this module can be added to their ICDL Professional learner profile.

For this book, it is recommended you have access to Microsoft Access 2016 or later as many of the core features described and illustrations used to involve the latest Microsoft 365 Access application using Windows on a PC. Many new additions to Microsoft Excel include cloud-based services such as OneDrive and newly added Ribbon display options. For this book, the core components covered in the Advanced Database exam can be used with earlier versions of Microsoft Access.

When I began learning advanced database, I often spent long moments scanning the groups, tabs, ribbons, and different buttons on-screen, searching for the correct function. I was familiar with the software's layout but struggled to use its less obvious features. The practical aspects of the application evaded me, and I became frustrated and disheartened. It was acquiring the skills and knowledge I needed to perform tasks effectively proved to be a long, laborious endeavour.

As I became familiar with its many advanced features, I found a more straightforward way of learning. Understand what I was doing, why it was necessary, and examples of how I might apply it to real-life situations. This is why I have written this book. I hope to share my knowledge with readers that may help them improve their existing skills using Microsoft Access.

It may seem daunting at first, but learn steps one at a time. If parts prove difficult, take note of it and move on, reviewing it later with a new perspective. I hope you find this book helpful and that you progress towards using Microsoft's other applications, including Word, Excel, and PowerPoint. Microsoft Access is only available for PC. The practical exercises outlined in this book are for Windows PC users.

Microsoft Access may be used for content management systems used in retail and e-commerce websites to keep track of inventory and customer details and companies who want to maintain records of clients, employees, and products.

Independent sole traders, entrepreneurs, administrative staff, managers, and retailers are just some of the business users of Microsoft Access. Advanced database skills allow readers to build on their current understanding of the application, enhance their career prospects, and make performing repetitive tasks easier and more efficient.

Students can also benefit from learning advanced database techniques. Whether they want to improve their knowledge of data entry settings, develop and maintain relationships between tables, create forms, and produce reports, acquiring the necessary skills required to do this is provided in this book.

How to use this book

I have divided the book into six parts, each one containing a number of easily navigable sections: Advanced Database, introduces you to these six parts:

Section 1 – Database Concepts. In this section, you will learn about different types of database models and stages, and their application to real-life situations.

Section 2 – Tables and Relationships. Learn how to create, edit, modify, and use tables of information in a database. Explore how relationships between tables form and how they affect data using links.

Section 3 – Queries. Discover how to request information from tables, and display results based on input with update, delete, and make-table queries.

Section 4 – Forms. Find out how to create, edit, and format parts of a form such as text boxes and calculated fields for other users.

Section 5 – Reports. This section explains how to create, edit, modify, and format elements in a report, such as cumulative sums, headers, footers, and subreports.

Section 6 – Enhancing Productivity. This final section covers linking and embedding data into worksheets such as spreadsheets, text files, and databases. Automating tasks with macros is also covered.

Now you know what to expect from the book, lets delve straight into Part One, Database Concepts

Contents

Section 1

Database Concepts

In this section, you will learn:

- Stages of a database

- Database models

- Real-life applications of databases

Types of Database Models

Databases store and access data in many ways. For example, companies use databases containing price and product information on an e-commerce site. Website content management systems allow database users to make changes to web content without having technical knowledge. Databases help businesses involved in distribution, logistics, shipping, and inventories. For example, a company may want to store customer data, such as contact details and home addresses, to be modified and updated.

Hierarchal databases are similar to a tree structure with records stored in groups of master and subordinate relationships. There may be a high priority table, e.g. containing customer details and relationships between many subordinate product tables. This model is fast and straightforward to use but only has one-to-many relationships.

Relational databases have data organised in a series of related tables. This type of database is easy to create, add to, and access. Companies use relational databases to manage employee details for different departments, such as employee name, salary, and department details. These details may be related to salary tables and managerial data sets.

Object-orientated databases have data represented by objects. Not all these models support Structured Query Language. SQL is a language used in Microsoft Access when it runs Queries.

Stages of a Database

Stage 1 – Design

The design must be clear and easy to understand. Consider the purpose of the database. How will it output data? What will the result of the database be? How will it serve the needs of the people who access it?

Stage 2 – Creation

Creation involves developing tables, relationships, forms, queries, and reports. This process needs careful attention to ensure a clear understanding of the links between tables and the output of selected databases.

Stage 3 – Data Entry

This stage involves entering information into a database. Data entry is a long, labour-intensive process and requires a skilled user. There are many features in Microsoft Access that can limit the chance of errors occurring, such as data validation methods that only allow specific information entry and input masks where data entered must be of a particular format.

Stage 4 – Data Maintenance

Data maintenance involves adding new information and removing unnecessary data from a database to make it more efficient. This process develops continually as information changes, e.g. contact details of customers or product updates.

Stage 5 – Information Retrieval

Information is retrieved and organised using queries, forms, and reports. Users may only be allowed to use sections of a database because of restrictions.

Applications of Databases

Databases serve the purpose of dynamic websites where data is retrieved and updated for information such as product details or prices. Databases manage mailing lists where e-mail details are stored. These databases can then be updated when contact details change.

For instance, when a customer enters contact details such as name, address, e-mail, and date of birth into a shopping website, this data is automatically retrieved and updated using company databases. This information relates to products purchased by that customer and is stored in the organisation's databases.

Website content management systems use databases where users without technical skills can edit information, e.g. product sales details. The user may input data without having to know coding languages. It makes data entry more effective and efficient.

Customer Relationship Management Systems uses databases to store and retrieve customer details in an organisation. A company can use information such as name and address. This information can then be updated whenever customers' details change.

This system may apply to a hotel business, for instance, where staff members use an established content management system. A client database may store guests' contact details. Information about the amount charged, length of stay and room stayed in may also be included in separate tables. This information can then be changed and updated as different guests arrive and leave the hotel.

Enterprise Resource Planning Systems are used in organisations regularly to perform functions such as accounting or finance. This database type may project sales forecasts, develop a company's budget, or track a department's financial position within a company. For instance, the accounts department may use this type of database to calculate the profit or loss of a company in a given year.

Structured Query Language

SQL is a coding language used in Microsoft Access that converts when queries run. This language applies to many computing platforms, including Azure and Microsoft's SQL Server. The average user would not need to know the SQL code behind queries, but it is useful to have knowledge of it.

1. Open the **Car Sales** database

2. Find the **Vehicles Query**

3. On the **Home** tab locate the **Views** group and select **Design View**

4. On the **Query Design** tab in the **Results** group, **Run** the query

5. Click the drop-down arrow on the **View** button and select **SQL View**

6. The **SQL** code for the query is displayed

7. The code contains information from the **Make**, **Model** and **Price** in the **Vehicles** table

8. The **Price** criteria are displayed

9. Click the **Close** button on the **Vehicles** Query tab to close the **SQL** view

10. Close the database

Revision Section 1

1. Name the three types of database models.

2. Give some examples of database applications.

3. What are the five stages of a database?

4. What are some of the applications of a database?

5. What is SQL, and what computing platforms use it?

Summary

Database Concepts

In this section, you have learned:

- Stages of a database including creation and design

- Database models such as relational and hierarchical

- Applications of databases including content management systems and e-commerce platforms

Section 2

Tables and Relationships

In this section, you will learn how to:

- Create, edit and modify tables

- Apply data entry settings

- Form different types of relationships between tables

Lookup in Fields/Columns

Users can type information into a field or lookup values from another table. A lookup field contains all the possible options for data entry. It can help to reduce typing mistakes as users can select an entry from a predefined list. You may apply settings to allow only entries from the list to appear.

1. Open the **Swift Cycles** database

2. Open the **Bicycles** table by right-clicking it and selecting **Design View**

3. After the field name **Telephone,** type in **Seller**

4. For **Data Type,** choose **Lookup Wizard**

5. Click on **I will type in the values that I want** and click **Next**

6. Set the **Number of Columns** as **1** and type in the following entries. Use the **Tab** key to move on to the next entry.

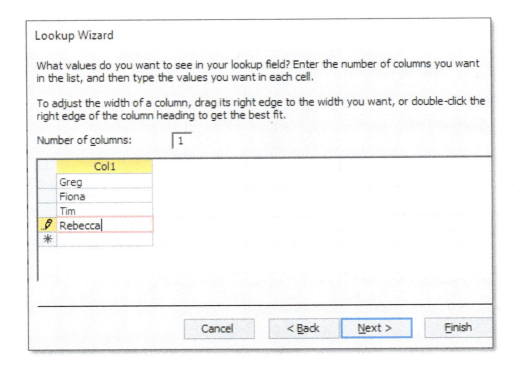

7. Click **Next.** Choose **Seller** as the label

8. Click **Finish** to create the **Lookup Field**

9. Change the view to **Datasheet** view and **Save** the table

10. In the **Seller** column, use the drop-down option to choose the following employees

11. Greg sold all the Velo bicycles, Fiona all the HBar bikes, Tim all the TechX bicycles and Rebecca the XCycles bikes

12. Return to **Design View** and select the **Lookup** tab in the **Field Properties** area for the **Seller** field name

13. Replace Tim with Mathew in the **Row Source** property by double-clicking on his name and typing in the new employee

14. Save the changes to the table and return to **Datasheet View**

15. Change the **Seller** records from Tim to Mathew

16. Save the table and leave it open

Input Masks

Input masks define how data is entered and shown in a field. Symbols define user input and how data is displayed. Input masks determine the format of the information entered into fields so that data will always appear in a table using the format decided by the user.

For example, if a table contains fields that require data entry for product numbers, an input mask of LL-0000-0 applies to records such as GJ-4857-9.

L = Letter (Required Entry)

? = Letter (Entry Not Required)

A = Letter or Number (Required Entry)

a = Letter or Number (Entry Not Required)

& = Any Character or Space (Required Entry)

C = Any Character or Space (Entry Not Required)

0 = Number (Required Entry)

9 = Number (Entry Not Required)

= Number, Space, + or –

., = Decimal Point and thousands separators

:/ = Date and time separators

< = Converts characters to the right to lowercase

> = Converts characters to the right to uppercase

\ = Makes the character that follows to be displayed as itself e.g. \H will be displayed as H

1. With the **Swift Cycles** database open, display the **Bicycles** table in **Design View**

2. Select the **Telephone** field

3. Under **Field Properties**, click in the **Input Mask** field property

4. Enter (00) 0000000 for the **Input Mask**

General	Lookup
Field Size	50
Format	
Input Mask	\(00") "0000000
Caption	
Default Value	
Validation Rule	
Validation Text	
Required	No
Allow Zero Length	Yes
Indexed	No
Unicode Compression	Yes
IME Mode	No Control
IME Sentence Mode	None
Text Align	General

5. Return to **Datasheet View** and try and enter a telephone number of (03) 6594857 for the record with a **Model Number** of 9478

6. The table will only accept telephone numbers in the **Input Mask** format

7. Display the **Design View**

8. Under **Field Properties** to the right of the **Input Mask** property, click on the dots. It will display the **Input Mask Wizard**

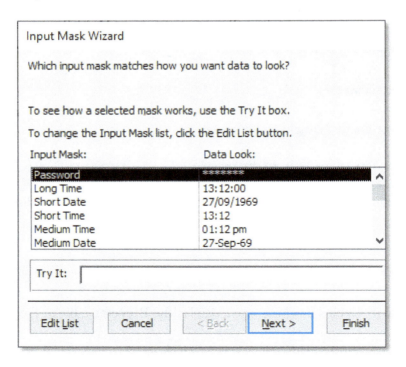

9. Scroll down through the list of **Input Masks** available until you reach the **Telephone** number **Input Mask**

10. Click on **Edit List**

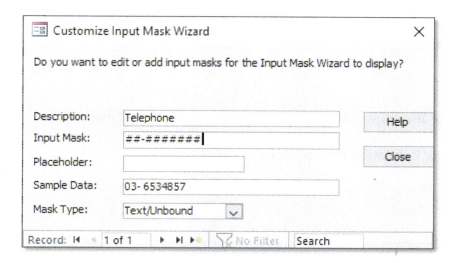

11. For **Input Mask** enter ##-########

12. Click on **Close**

13. Click on **Next**

14. Click **Finish**

15. When you return to **Datasheet View**, it applies the **Input Mask** of the **Telephone** field

16. Save the database and leave it open

Setting Data Entry

Some fields are essential to a database. Without some fields, the database may not function properly, e.g. customer titles such as Mr or Ms Field properties can be set as required. It means that information entry is required, and it will be impossible to add a new record without data. It reduces the possibility of errors occurring so the database functions correctly.

1. With the **Bicycles** table open in **Design View**, select the **Title** field

2. Select the **Validation Rule** property

3. Type in Mr Or Mrs Or Ms Or Miss

4. It will establish data entry for this field

General Lookup	
Field Size	50
Format	
Input Mask	
Caption	
Default Value	
Validation Rule	"Mr" Or "Mrs" Or "Ms" Or "Miss"
Validation Text	Enter Mr or Mrs or Ms or Miss
Required	Yes
Allow Zero Length	Yes
Indexed	No
Unicode Compression	Yes
IME Mode	No Control
IME Sentence Mode	None
Text Align	General

5. Click inside the **Required** property and select **Yes** from the options available

6. It will make an entry required in this field

7. Type the text "Enter Mr or Mrs or Ms or Miss" for the **Validation Text** property

8. Save the table and return to **Datasheet** view

9. Try entering "Sir" for the customer **Daniel**

10. An error message will appear displaying the validation text

11. Click **OK**

12. Return to **Design View**

13. Select the **Required** property and select **No** from the options available

14. Leave the **Title** for the first record blank

15. Access allows this as input is not required

16. Save the table and keep it open

Table Relationships

Relationships link tables together using a Primary Key in the primary table. It denotes a common field shared between a primary table and a secondary table. The secondary table, which shares a common field with the primary table, is a Foreign Key.

The primary and foreign keys are common fields, e.g. both may be titled "Address". The primary table, e.g. customers, contains customer addresses and the secondary table, e.g. products, also contain customer addresses.

A One-to-One relationship is where one record in one table links to only one record in another table. A One-to-Many relationship is where one record in one table links to many related records in another table.

1. Open the **Swift Cycles** database

2. Click on the **Database Tools** tab

3. Select the **Relationships** button

4. In the **Relationships** group, select **Add Tables**

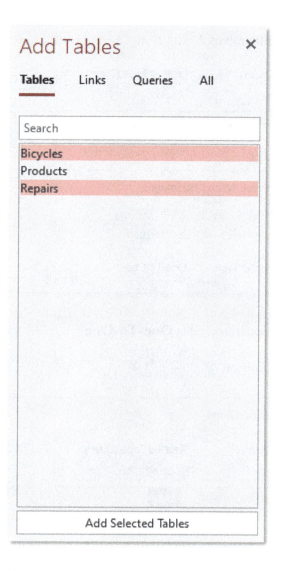

5. Hold down the **Ctrl** key and select the **Bicycles** table

6. Select the **Repairs** table

7. Choose **Add Selected Tables**

8. Click and drag on the **Model Number** field from the **Bicycles** table over to the **Model Number** field on the **Repairs** table

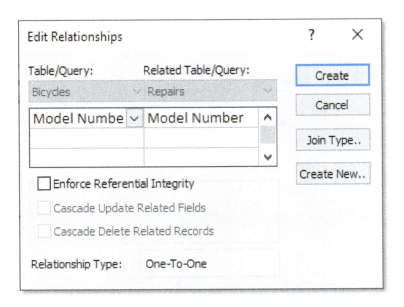

9. Notice how the relationship type is **One-To-One**

10. Click on the **Cancel** button

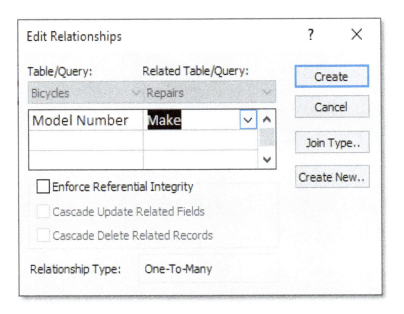

11. Click and drag the **Model Number** to the **Make** field

12. Notice now how the relationship type is **One-To-Many**

13. Click **Create** to create the relationship. A **One-To-Many** relationship forms between both tables

14. Save the table and leave it open

Many-to-Many Relationship

A Many-to-Many relationship forms when a record in the first table can have many matching records in the second table or when the second table can have many matching records in the first table.

For example, on an e-commerce website, a customer may have one order with several different products, and a single product may have many orders. It will have three linked tables, customers, products, and orders.

A Many-to-Many relationship cannot exist on its own. You create a related junction table with one-to-many links to the two main tables. It could be the products table. It must contain two fields with the foreign keys from both tables.

1. Open the **Swift Cycles** database

2. You must create an intermediate table to form a Many-to-Many relationship between the **Bicycles** and **Products** tables

3. Add the **Products** table to the **Relationships** window

4. You must create a primary key for the **Repairs** table with both the **Model Number** and **Product Ref** fields

5. Open the **Repairs** table in **Design View**

6. Click and drag to the left of the **Model Number** and **Product Ref** fields to select both

7. On the **Table** Design tab, in the **Tools** group, apply a **Primary Key** to both fields by clicking on the **Primary Key**

8. Save the table and close it

9. Open the **Relationships** window

10. Click and drag the **Product Ref** field from the **Repairs** table to the **Products** table

11. A **One-to-Many** relationship between the **Repairs** table and the **Products** table has formed

12. There has been a **Many-to-Many** relationship created between the **Bicycles** and **Products** tables due to the two **One-to-Many** relationships.

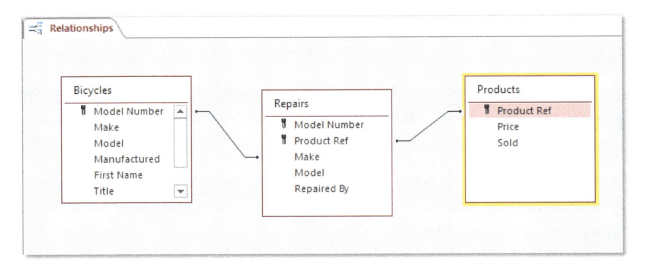

13. Save the database and leave it open

Referential Integrity

Referential integrity is when rules to relationships with specific conditions are applied, e.g. data are not accidentally deleted or changed. It will ensure that the relationships are valid, making the database function effectively. If a database user changes information in one table, this may affect the information contained in another table, thus making the database dysfunctional.

1. Open the **Swift Cycles** database and display the **Relationships** between the tables

2. Right-click on the relationship line between the **Bicycles** and **Repairs** table and select **Edit Relationship**

3. Ensure you select the **Model Number** fields for the relationship between both tables

4. In the **Edit Relationship** dialog box, select the checkbox **Enforce Referential Integrity**

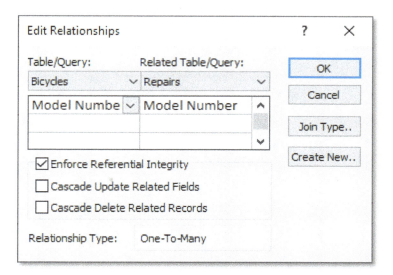

5. Click **OK**

6. Open the **Bicycles** table in **Datasheet View**

7. Select the record containing **Model Number** 2948

8. Right-click on the record and choose **Delete Record**

9. You may not delete the record because there are related records in the **Repairs** table

10. Click **OK**

11. Right-click on the record containing **Model Number** 2938

12. It is allowed as there are no corresponding records contained in the **Repairs** table

13. Leave the database open

Automatic Field Update

You may apply a setting to update fields in a database automatically. Automatic field updates are useful for updating records when fields in related tables are changed. It also allows the deletion of records reflecting changes in associated tables.

1. Open the **Relationships** window

2. Right-click on the relationship line between the **Bicycles** table and the **Repairs** table

3. Select **Edit Relationship**

4. Select the checkboxes **Cascade Update Related Fields** and **Cascade Delete Related Records**

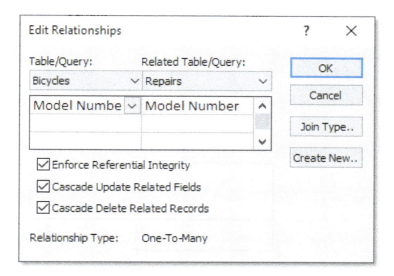

6. Click **OK**. This setting allows changes to be made in one table and reflected in the others

7. Close the **Relationships** window

8. Open the **Bicycles** table in **Datasheet View**

9. Delete the record containing **Model Number 3948**

10. A prompt will appear informing you that deletion in the related **Repairs** table occurs

11. Click **Yes** on the warning dialog box

12. Open the **Repairs** table

13. Notice how the same record containing **Model Number 3948** no longer appears in the related table

14. Display the **Bicycles** table in **Datasheet View**

15. Enter the following information:

Model Number	3647
Make	XCycles
Model	G570
Manufactured	2018
First Name	Harold
Title	Mr
Address	45 Main Street
Telephone	01-3746548
Seller	Fiona

16. Save the table and open the **Repairs** table

17. Access will prompt you to allow the addition of a new record. Select **Yes**

18. Click on the **Plus** sign to the left of the record

19. It displays the **Subdatasheet** containing information related to the **Repairs** table

20. Include a **Product Ref** of 334 and have the bicycle repaired by **Fiona,** including the same details contained within the **Bicycles** table

21. **Close the Repairs** table and re-open it

22. The new record appears in the **Repairs** table

23. Save the table and the database and leave it open

Inner & Outer Join

Joins are links between tables that determine how queries select records between related tables. An inner join only displays records with a corresponding entry in both tables. For example, a query on linked Bicycles and Repairs tables would only show bicycles that had a repair. Any bicycles without repairs would not be displayed. If you wanted to display all bicycles in a query regardless of whether they had a match in the Repairs table, you would change the link to an outer join or subtract join based on the Bicycles table. It would show all repair records. A table with a join with itself is a self-join.

1. Open the **Swift Cycles** database and open the **Bicycles** table.

2. Create a new record containing the following information: **3847, TechX, i350, 2017, Louise, Ms., 46 Main Street, (03) 4657483, Mathew**

3. Close the table.

4. Double-click on the relationship line between the **Bicycles** table and the **Repairs** table

5. Click on **Join Type**

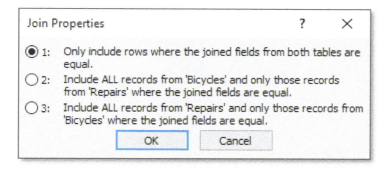

6. Notice how the join type only includes rows where the joined fields from both tables are equal. It is an **inner join.**

7. Select the second option. It will include all records from the **Bicycles** table and only the records from the **Repairs** table where the joined fields are equal. It is an **outer join**.

8. Click **OK** and click **OK** again

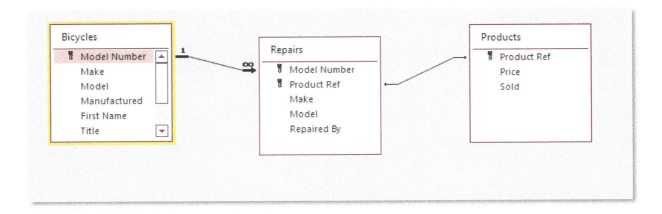

9. The relationship changes to a right-facing arrow identifying it as an **Outer Join**

10. Save the **Relationships** window and any remaining open tables

11. Close the database

Revision Section 2

1. Open the **College** database

2. Apply an **Input Mask** to the **Price** field in the **Courses** table that will use a **Currency** symbol with two decimal places

3. Apply a **Validation Rule** for the **Title** field in the **Teachers** table that will only allow data entry of titles' Mr' 'Mrs' or 'Ms'

4. Add a **Primary Key** to **Course ID** in the **Courses** table and **Teacher ID** in the **Teachers** table

5. Create a **One-to-One** relationship between both tables using the **Course ID** field

6. **Enforce Referential Integrity** and **Cascade** options

7. Update the **Teachers** table by adding a new record with the following information:

   127, Tom, Gregory, 164 Glenview Park, (01) 3647384

8. Apply an **Outer Join** to the relationship between both tables

9. Remove **Cascade** options in the **Relationship** between both tables

10. Delete the new record from the **Teachers** table

11. For teacher **Paula Dunne** use the **Subdatasheet** to change the course duration to **32 Weeks**

12. Open the **Courses** table and notice the change made to the course duration

13. Save the relationships and tables

14. Close the database

Summary

Tables & Relationships

In this section, you have learned:

- Data input and adjusting field settings

- Data validation and input masks for tables

- Table relationships using inner, outer, and subtract joins

Section 3

Queries

In this section, you will learn how to:

- Create make-table, append and delete queries

- Perform calculations using formulae in queries

- Prompt users to enter information with variable parameter queries

Update Query

An update query will update a chosen field in a table or several tables. This feature includes additional information in a table when it is required. For example, when you want to change the name of a product, an update query applies.

1. Open the **Orders** database

2. Open the **Products** table in **Datasheet View** and notice the number of records contained within the table

3. Display the **Create** tab and locate the **Queries** group, select **Query Design**

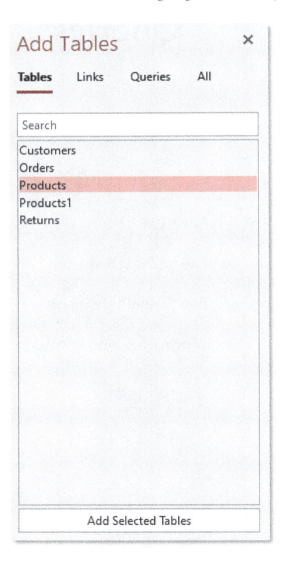

4. On the **Add Tables** pane, select the **Products** table and click on the **Add Selected Tables** button

5. The **Products** table fields involve the query

6. On the **Query Design** tab in the **Query Type** group, select **Update**

7. Include the **Product** and **Price** fields in the query

8. For the **Price** field, in the **Update To:** property, enter **[price]*0.8** and in **Criteria,** enter **>350**

Field:	Product	Price
Table:	Products	Products
Update To:		[price]*0.8
Criteria:		> 350
or:		

9. It will apply a 20% discount for all products over €350

10. On the **Query Design** tab in the **Results** group, click on **Run**

11. It will carry out the query according to the criteria set

12. Click **Yes** when prompted to update four rows

13. View the **Products** table in **Datasheet View**

14. Notice the four additional records added to the table

15. Save the query as **20% Discount**

16. Leave the database open

Append Records

An append query selects a group of records from a table and adds them to the end of another table. The original table remains unchanged. This feature allows you to include data that meet specified criteria at the end of another table. For example, a company may want to add new customers to its tables in a database. An append query applies to this requirement.

1. Open the **Orders** database

2. Display the **Create** tab and locate the **Queries** group, select **Query Design**

3. Add the **Returns** table to the query

4. This query will search the **Returns** table and select the orders with a **Customer ID** beginning with **CR**. The records add to the **Customers** table

5. On the **Design** tab, locate the **Query Type** group, select **Append**

6. The **Append** dialog box appears. Select **Customers** for **Table Name**

7. Select the **Current Database** option

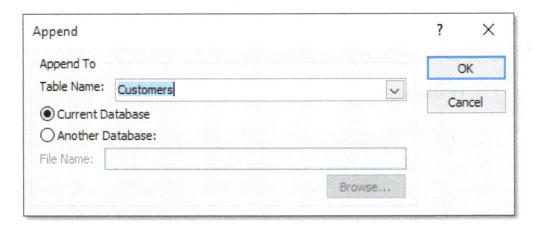

8. Click **OK**. The **Append To:** row appears on the query grid

9. Click and drag the **Customer ID** field onto the grid.

10. Click and drag the **Title, First Name, Surname** & **Address** fields onto the query grid

11. These fields are in the **Customers** table, so it will be possible to add this information to that table

12. In the **Criteria** row in the **Customer ID** field, enter **CR***. The **Asterix** is a **Wildcard** character. It will add only fields with a **Customer ID** beginning with **CR**

13. Run the query

14. A dialog box will appear informing you that you are about to append two rows of data. Click **OK**

15. Open the **Customers** table. Notice the two additional records included in the table beginning with the **Customer ID** of **CR**

16. Save the query as **Customer Returns**

17. Close the table and the query

18. Leave the database open

Delete Query

A delete query will delete a selected collection of records from one or more tables. The query removes records from the original table. A delete query could be performed after an append query when the records from the original table need deletion. For instance, if a company wants to remove a product from its database, it can perform a delete query that removes records related to that product.

1. With the **Orders** database open

2. Display the **Create** tab and locate the **Queries** group, click on **Query Design**

3. Add the **Returns** table to the query

4. On the **Design** tab, locate the **Query Type** group, select the **Delete** option

5. Click and drag the **Customer ID, Title, First Name, Surname & Address** fields from the **Returns** table to the query grid

6. In the **Customer ID** field, enter **Like "CR*"** to the **Criteria** row

Field:	Customer ID	Title	First Name	Surname	Address
Table:	Returns	Returns	Returns	Returns	Returns
Delete:	Where	Where	Where	Where	Where
Criteria:	Like "CR*"				
or:					

7. On the **Query Design** tab in the **Results** group, click on **Run** to perform the query

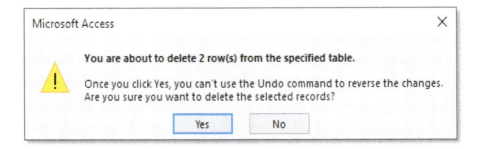

8. A dialog box informing you that you will delete two rows from the selected table will appear. Click **Yes**

9. Save the query as **TV Returned**

10. Open the **Returns** table. Notice that only the customer who returned the television appears in the table

11. Close the table and leave the database open

Make-Table Query

A make-table query selects data from one or more tables and creates a new table from that data. With this type of query, you choose what fields to include in the new table. It is possible to choose a selection of fields from several tables to create a new table.

For example, a company may have a products table, an orders table, and a customers table in a database. You can retrieve information about customers who have ordered certain products over the age of 30, using a make-table query to display customers who meet these criteria in a new table.

1. Open the **Orders** database

2. Display the **Create** tab and locate the **Queries** group, select **Query Design**

3. Add the **Orders** and **Products** tables to the query

4. On the **Design** tab, locate the **Query Type** group, select **Make Table**

5. Call the Table Name **Customer Orders**

6. Select the **Current Database** option

7. Click **OK**

8. Click and drag the **Product ID** field from the **Products** table onto the query grid

9. Place the **Price** and **Paid** fields from the **Orders** table onto the query grid

10. For the **Criteria** in the **Paid** field, type in "Yes"

11. For the **Criteria** in the **Price** field, type in "<200"

12. Save the query as **Paid Products <200**

13. Run the query

14. It will create a new table with all customers who have paid for products under €200

15. Double-click on the **Customer Orders** table

16. It creates a table using the **Make-Table** query by displaying customers who paid under €200 for products

17. Close the table and leave the database open

Crosstab Query

A crosstab query shows summarised values such as Sum, Avg, Count, Max, etc., for fields within a table or query and groups them together. The columns and rows of the display contain fields from the table or query. The query contents contain the calculated fields based on the fields selected, e.g. the average price. Crosstab queries can either be created manually or using a wizard.

For example, a store may want to find the total income generated from sales. The shop uses a crosstab query that summarises the total value of products sold using the Sum calculation.

1. Open the **Orders** database

2. Display the **Create** tab and locate the **Queries** group, select **Query Wizard**

3. Select **Crosstab Query Wizard** and click **OK**

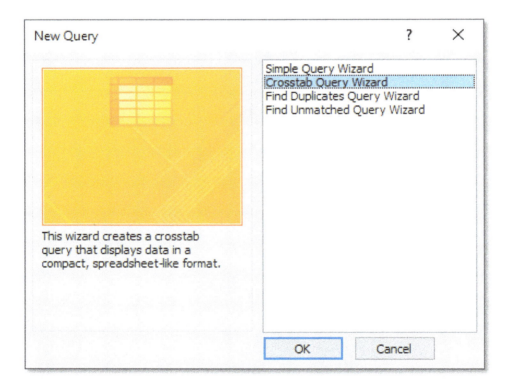

4. Choose the **Orders** table

5. Select to view **Tables** and click **Next**

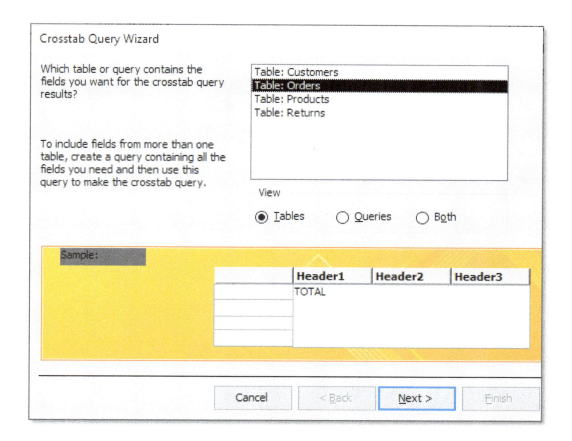

6. From the **Available Fields**, select **Product**

7. Click on the **Right-facing arrow** to add the **Product** field for the **Row Headings**

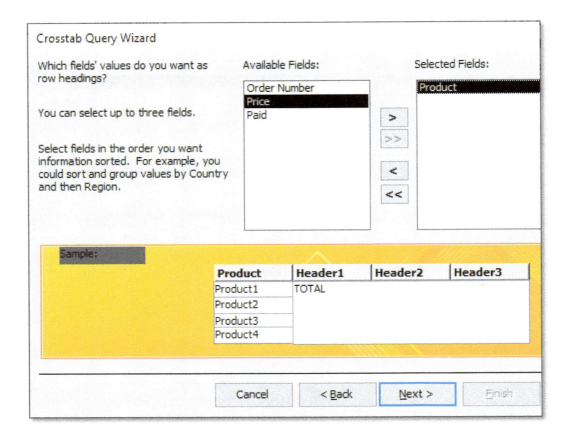

8. Click **Next**

9. Choose **Order Number** for the column headings

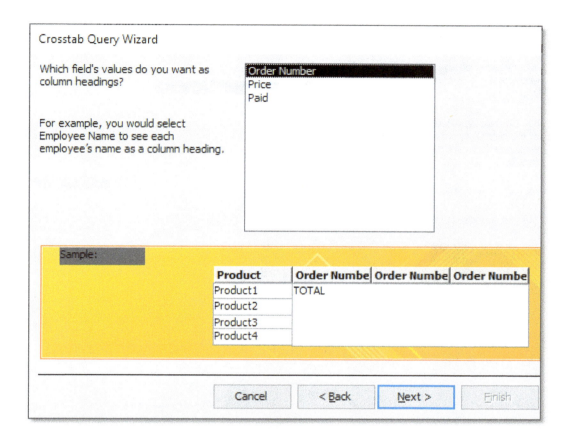

10. Click on **Next**

11. Choose **Price** for the **Sum** function

12. Leave the **Yes, include rows sums** checkbox and click **Next**

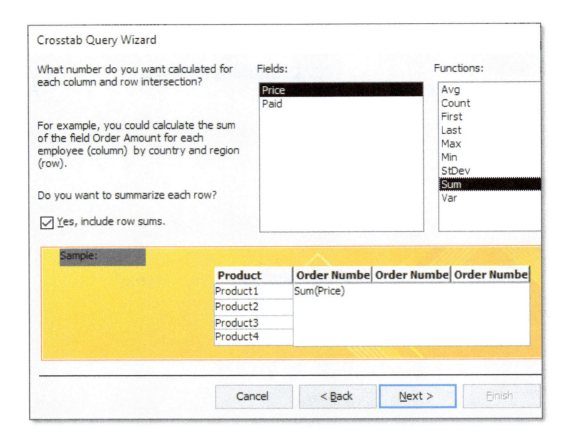

13. Name the query **Products Table**

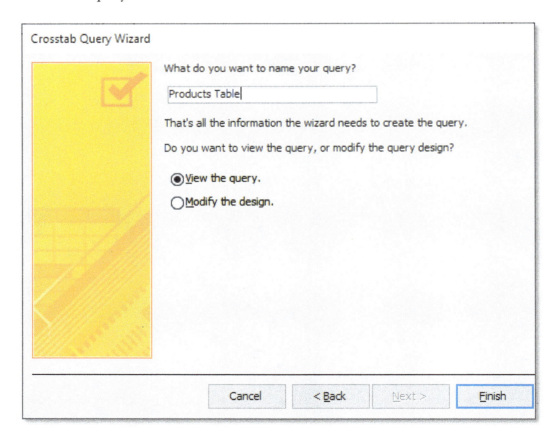

14. Choose to **View the Query** and select **Finish**

15. The **Crosstab Query** creates a table similar to a spreadsheet

16. The column headers contain the **Order Numbers,** the row headers will include the **Product Name,** and the **Total of Price** column consists of the **Sum Total Price** for each product

17. Save the table and close it, leaving the database open

Duplicated Records

A find duplicates query will search a table for duplicate records. A find duplicates query displays duplicate records automatically. It is a helpful feature that checks data entered twice accidentally. For example, whenever there are mistakes made during data entry and information is accidentally entered two or more times.

1. Open the **Orders** database

2. On the **Create** tab, locate the **Queries** group, select **Query Wizard**

3. Select **Find Duplicates Query Wizard** and click **OK**

4. Select the **Customers Table** and choose to display the duplicates query as a **Table**

5. Click **Next**

6. Add the **First Name, Surname** & **Address** fields by selecting each field and clicking on the **right-hand arrow** to add them as **Duplicate-Value Fields**

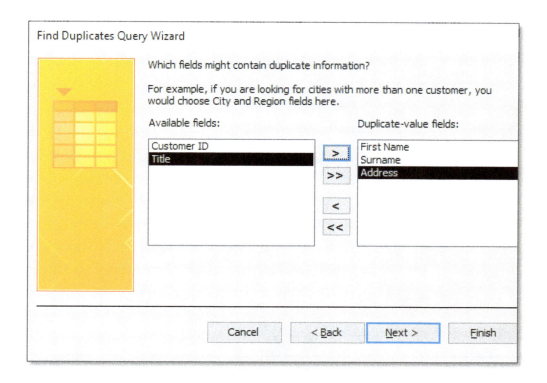

7. Both fields need to match before counting records as duplicates. Click **Next**

8. Select the **Customer ID** & **Title** as additional query fields and click on the **double right-facing arrow** to add the fields

9. It will show fields with single values as well as fields containing duplicate values

10. Click **Next**, name the query as **Duplicate Customer Details** and click **Finish**

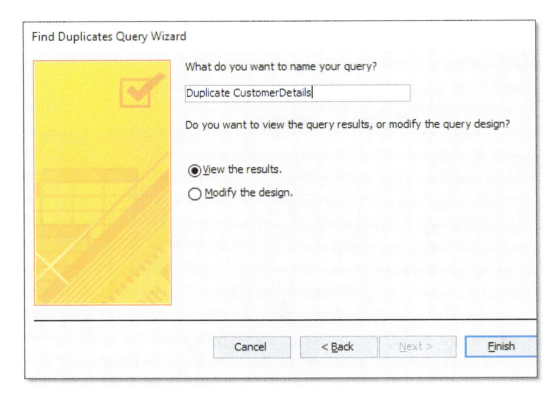

11. The query will run and show the duplicate fields contained within the **Customers** table

12. The customer record "Sarah Walsh" appears in the table

13. Save the query and leave the database open

Unmatched Records

The find unmatched query finds records in a table not included in another table. For example, in an adult learning centre, there may be a Teacher's table containing contact details of each teacher with no records held in a linked Classes table. Using a find unmatched query can automatically display Teacher records that do not match those contained in the linked Classes tables.

1. Open the **Orders** database

2. On the **Create** tab, locate the **Queries** group, click on **Query Wizard**

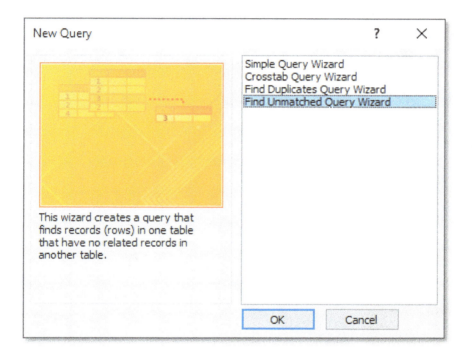

3. Select **Find Unmatched Query Wizard** and click **OK**

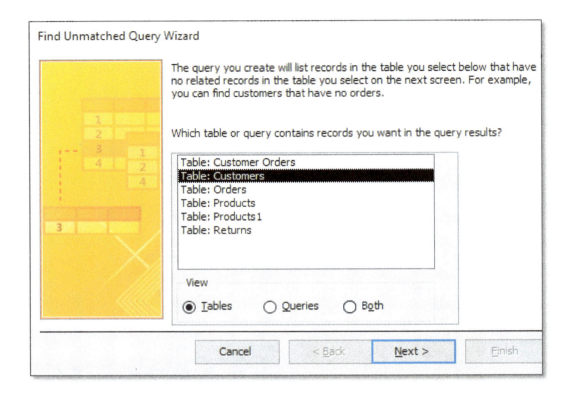

4. Choose the **Customers** table to include in the query and select **Tables** under **View**

5. Click **Next**

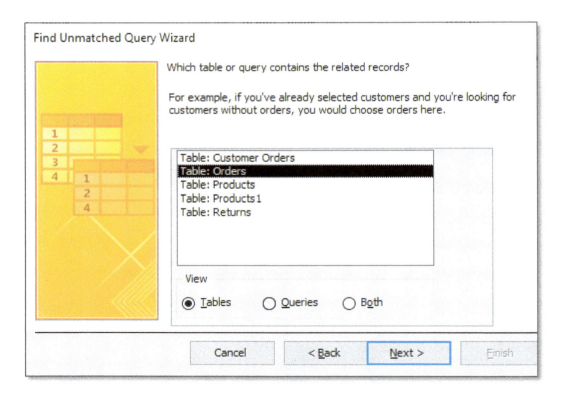

6. Select the **Orders** table. It is where you are trying to find customers <u>without</u> orders

7. Click **Next**

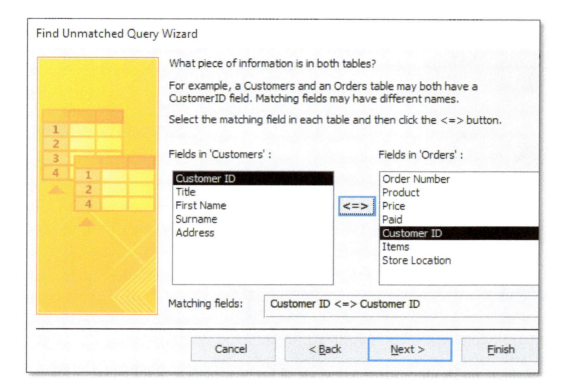

8. Select the **Customer ID** for both tables and click on the **Directional Arrow Button**

9. The **Matching Fields** textbox appears with **Customer ID** for both tables

10. Click **Next**

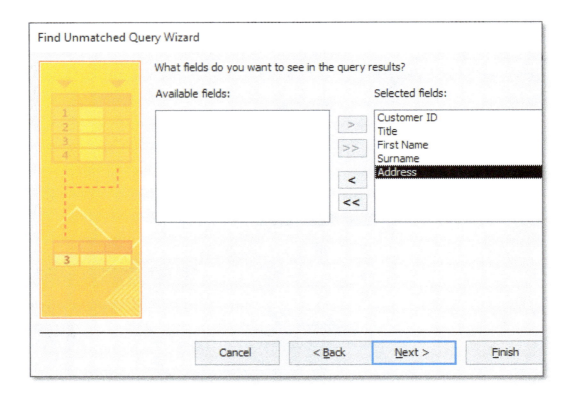

11. Click on the **Double-Arrow** to include all fields as the **Selected Fields**

12. Click **Next**

13. Name the query **Customers Without Orders** and click **Finish**

14. Customers without orders are displayed

15. Save the query and close it

Variable Parameter Query

A variable parameter query displays a dialog box prompting you to enter information. When you enter specific information, the query runs. The next time a query runs, you enter a different value using the same query.

For example, a variable parameter query may prompt the database user to display the address of customers in an area. Access prompts you to type in the city, e.g. London. The query shows all the customers who live in London.

Parameter queries work with other types of queries, including make-table queries. A query can contain as many parameter values as is needed. Each time the query runs, a dialog box will appear for each field with a parameter value.

1. Open the **Orders** table

2. Display the **Create** tab and locate the **Queries** group, select **Query Design**

3. Add the **Customers** table

4. Click and drag the **First Name, Surname** & **Address** fields onto the query grid

5. In the **Address** field, type in: **[Enter Location]** with **Square Brackets** as the **Criteria**

6. On the **Query Design** tab in the **Results** group, select **Run**

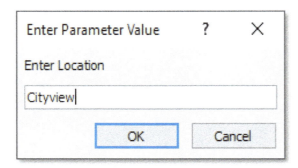

7. A prompt appears to enter customers' location

8. Type in **Cityview** and click **OK**

9. The query will display all the customers with an address in **Cityview**

10. Save the query as **Cityview Customers** and close it

11. Double-click on the **Cityview Customers** query on the **Access Objects** pane

12. A dialog box appears, prompting you to enter a location

13. Type in **Glenview**

14. All customers living in **Glenview** will appear

15. It is a **One Variable Parameter Query** as it has one changeable setting

16. Save the query as Cityview **Customers** and close it

Wildcards

Wildcards find matching text in a table. The wildcards replace a letter or group of letters when entering text. Wildcards search tables when the actual text of the records are unknown, e.g. C*, to search for records beginning with C.

More specific searches may find records containing specified names, e.g. City????. It may display an address beginning with City and contains four letters such as Cityview or Cityside.

When the database user wants to find product ID records that include numbers, they may use wildcards such as GR-####-A. It will search the table for records, e.g. GR-5847-A.

You may use the following characters for wildcards:

? = stands for a single alphabetic character

= stands for a single numeric character

* = represents any group of characters

[!ao]* = omits chosen characters or numbers, e.g. does not display records containing the letter a or o

1. Open the **Orders** table

2. Display the **Create** tab and locate the **Queries** group, click on **Query Design**

3. Add the **Customers** table

4. Click and drag all fields onto the query grid

5. In the **Criteria** for **Surname**, type **D?***

6. **Run** the query

7. The query displays customers with a surname beginning with D

8. Delete the **Criteria** and enter the following information: **D[!aio]***

9. Inside the **Square Brackets** after the letter **D** enter an **Exclamation Mark** followed by the letters AIO and include an **Asterix** outside of the **Square Brackets**

10. It will display all the customer surnames that begin with D but does <u>not</u> contain the letter A, I or O

11. Run the query

12. Two records for **Mark Dunne** appear based on the queries criteria

13. Return to **Design View** and delete the contents of the surname **Criteria**

14. On the **Customer ID** field, enter the **Criteria** as Like "C3##"

15. Run the query. It will display all the customers who have a **Customer ID** that begins with the characters C3

16. Five records appear as the output of the query

17. On the **Customer ID** field, enter the **Criteria** W[!eio]*

18. After the letter **W** put an **Exclamation Mark** with the letters EIO inside **Square Brackets** with an **Asterix** after the final bracket

19. **Run** the query

20. The query produces two records for the customer **Sarah Walsh** as the **Customer ID** begins with C3 and the **Surname** begins with W without the letters EIO

21. Save the query as **Wildcards** and close it

Maximum and Minimum Values

Max and Min are calculations used in a query that show the maximum and minimum values of selected fields. The TopValues property displays a range of the highest and lowest values in a table. It shows records that fall within specific ranges, such as prices for a product that are between €500 and €1,000

1. Open the **Orders** database

2. Display the **Create** tab and locate the **Queries** group, click on **Query Design**

3. Add the **Orders** table and include the **Product, Paid** & **Price** fields. Include the **Price** fields twice

4. It will allow you to compare price ranges using a query

5. Right-click on the first **Price** field and select **Totals**. It will display the **Total** row

Field:	Product	Paid	Price	Price	
Table:	Orders	Orders	Orders	Orders	
Total:	Group By	Group By	Max	Min	⌄
Sort:					
Show:	☑	☑	☑	☑	
Criteria:					
or:					

6. Click on the **Drop-down Arrow** with the name **Group By**

7. Select **Max** for the first **Price** field in the **Total** row and **Min** for the second **Price** field

8. In the **Sort** row, click on the drop-down arrow and select **Ascending** for the **Max Price** column

9. On the **Query Design** tab in the **Query Setup** group for **Return,** click on the drop-down arrow and choose **25%**

10. **Run** the query

11. It displays the **Maximum** and **Minimum** prices of the **25%** cheapest products

12. In this case, two products appear

13. Save the query as **Cheapest Quarter Products** and close it

Calculated Field

A calculated field shows the results of a calculation. The calculation may have more numerical fields and include logical or mathematical calculations. Calculated fields can multiply two fields, add fields, subtract one field from another, and divide. If statements involve calculated fields to determine whether field values meet specific criteria.

Calculated fields include the Add + symbol, Subtract -, Multiply *, and Divide / symbols

1. Open the **Orders** database

2. Display the **Create** tab and locate the **Queries** group, select **Query Design** and add the **Orders** table

3. Click and drag every field in the **Orders** table onto the query grid

4. In the blank field row where names for each column are displayed, to the right of **Store Location,** type in the following formula:

   Total Sold: [Price]*[Items]

5. It will multiply the **Price** of a product by the number of **Items** sold, giving you a calculated field containing the **Total Sold**

6. Run the query and notice the calculated total amount for each product

7. You may use logical expressions in queries. Return to **Design View**. To the right of the **Total Sold** calculation, type in the following expression (Include **IIf** for the **IF** statement and only include a space between **Cost**: and **IIf**):

   Profit: IIf([Total Sold]>300,"Profitable","Not Profitable")

8. Enter 300 into the **Total Sold** dialog box when prompted and click **OK**

9. It will display the word "Profitable" for order totals above €300 and the words "Not Profitable" for order totals lower than €300 for the company

10. Save the query as **Calculated Sales** and close it

Sum Functions

The sum function adds values in a field together. It shows a summary calculation within a query rather than a single calculation for each record. This function can find the total amount out of a range of records. For example, in a staff list for a company, if you want to find the total amount spent on salaries, the sum function displays this calculation.

1. Open the **Orders** database

2. Display the **Create** tab and locate the **Queries** group, select **Query Design**

3. Add the **Orders** table

4. Click and drag the **Store Location** and **Price** fields onto the query grid

5. Right-click on the query grid and select **Totals**

6. In the **Total** row with the label **Group By**, select **Sum** from the drop-down box for the **Price** field

7. **Run** the query

8. It displays the total amount spent in each store

9. Save the query as **Store Income** and close it

Count Functions

The count function counts a specified number of fields. It is a summary calculation that counts selected values in a field and summarises the information contained within a table. For example, you may want to determine the total number of products sold in an orders table. A count function produces the total amount of products.

1. Open the **Orders** database

2. Display the **Create** tab and locate the **Queries** group, select **Query Design**

3. Add the **Orders** table

4. Include **Store Location** and **Items** onto the query grid

5. Right-click on the query grid and select **Totals**

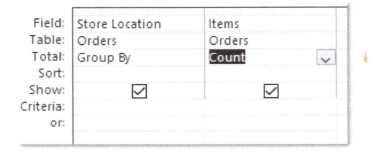

6. For the **Total** row labelled **Group By** in the **Items** field, choose **Count**

7. Run the query. It has calculated the total number of product items sold in each store location

8. Save the query as **Store Items Sold** and close it

Average Function

The avg function calculates the average of all values in a field. A summary value displays the average out of a range of values within a table. It is a useful function to use when finding the average out of a set of values. A car mechanics company may want to calculate the average cost of repairs for vehicles requiring specific jobs, such as a car service. The average function can calculate the average cost of repairs.

1. Open the **Orders** database

2. Display the **Create** tab and locate the **Queries** group, select **Query Design**

3. Add the **Orders** table

4. Click and drag the **Store Location** field onto the query grid and place the **Price** and the **Paid** field next to it

5. Right-click on the query grid and select **Totals**

6. In the **Price** field, **Total** row labelled **Group By**, select **Avg** from the drop-down box

7. In the **Criteria** row of the **Paid** field, type in **Yes.** It finds the average of all the paid-for items

8. **Run** the query. A query will be displayed showing the average price of products sold categorised by store location

9. Save the query as **Average Sales** and close it

Revision Section 3

1. Open the **Orders** database

2. Create an **Update Query** based on the **Products** table showing the **Product** and **Price** fields that will apply a 15% discount for products over €200 and save it as **Discount**

3. Create an **Append Query** that will add table records from the **Products** table containing a **Product** containing the word **Television** to the **Customers Orders** table. Include the **Product ID**, **Price**, & **Product** fields. Save the query as **Customer Products**

4. Create a **Delete Query** that will remove all the records containing **Notebook** from the **Products** table. Display **Product ID**, **Product**, & **Price** fields. Save the query as **Deleted Records.**

5. Create a **Make-Table Query** to create a table containing all the products in stock above €200. Name the table **Products Over 200** and include the **Order Number, Product** and **Price** fields from the **Products** table. Save the query as **Product Orders**

6. Create a **Crosstab** query based on the **Orders** table That will display the **Average** price for each **Product** based on its **Order Number.** Save the table as **Average Price** and close it

7. Create a **Variable Parameter Query** based on the **Customers** table with the **First Name** and **Address** fields that prompt users to enter a location. Enter **Glenview** for the location and run the query. Save the query as **Glenview Customers** and close it

8. Create a query based on the **Orders** table displaying each field that uses a calculation that shows a new field titled **Profit** that will display the word **"High"** for totals over €400 and **"Low"** for totals under €400. Save the query as **Profit** and close it

9. Close the database

Summary

Queries

In this section, you have learned:

- Make-table, append, delete and update queries

- Sum, average and IIF statement calculations

- Single and double parameter queries

Section 4

Forms

In this section, you will learn how to:

- Create, edit and format forms

- Embed subforms into main forms

- Create and apply settings to form elements

Text Box

A text box creates a label and a text box in a form. It creates a label and displays calculations in the text box.

Bound form controls obtain data from a source in the database such as a field, e.g. a calculation for total departmental sales.

Unbound form controls are not linked to a data source and perform calculations independently, e.g. total sales for a company using totals from each department.

Calculations can use any mathematical symbols (+, -, *, /) and expressions such as Average, Sum, Max, and Min. If statements perform calculations based on certain criteria, e.g. if employee salaries are above €24,000, add them together, if not, do not add.

1. Open the **Computer Store** database

2. Open the **Products Form**

3. Enlarge the **Details** area by clicking and dragging the separator labelled **Details**

4. On the **Form Design** tab in the **Controls** group, click on the **Text Box** button

5. Create a **Text Box** by clicking and dragging where you want it to appear

6. It creates an **Unbound Control** separate from other text boxes

7. On the **Form Design** tab in the **Tools** group, select **Property Sheet** to display the control's properties

8. The **Property Sheet** pane appears

9. Click on the **Data** tab on the **Property Sheet** pane and locate the **Control Source** property

10. Click on the drop-down arrow and choose **Product** as the **Control Source**

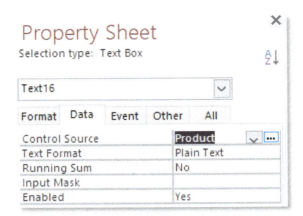

11. The source of the calculation is the **Product**

12. This textbox is now a **Bound Control** as the calculation links to the **Product** field

13. Click on the **Other** tab on the **Property Sheet** pane and locate the **Name**.property

14. Enter in **Product_Total** for the **Name** property

15. Enter the following formula into the text box:

    =[Price]*[Items Sold]

16. On the **Home** tab in the **Text Formatting** group, click on the **Left Alignment** button to align the value to the left of the text box

17. On the **Property Sheet** pane, click on the **Format** tab

18. Change the **Decimal Places** to **0** using the drop-down box

19. Name the label **Product Total**

20. Reposition the label and text box by clicking and dragging the grey box on the top left-hand corner of the label

21. Click and drag the edges of the label and calculated field to align them with the **Items Sold** label above

22. Reposition the label while holding down the **Ctrl** key to move only the **Product Total** label

23. Click inside the text box, and on the **Property Sheet** pane, select the **Format** tab

24. From the drop-down options, change the format to **Euro**

25. On the **Form Design** tab in the **Views** group, click on the downward-facing arrow to select **Form View**

26. Click on the arrows at the bottom of the screen to move through each record

27. On the **Home** tab in the **Views** group, click on the downward-facing arrow to return to **Design View**

28. Enlarge the **Detail** area to create more space for the new **Unbound Control** text box

29. Add another text box under the **Product Total**

30. Enter in the following expression in the text box:

    =IIf([Product_Total]>1000,"High Value","Low Value")

31. This expression will show the text "High Value" if the product total is above €1,000 and display "Low Value" if the product total is lower than €1,000

32. Enter a label of **Product Value**

33. Rearrange the label and text box to align them with the **Product Total** calculation above

34. Switch to **Form View** and move through each record

35. Notice the values appearing in the **Product Value** text box

36. Save the form and close it

Combo Box

A combo box is a field on a form that allows you to choose from a drop-down list. It is often seen when ordering the colour of an item of clothing on a clothing company website, for instance. It will prevent the incorrect entry of data when filling in a form. Create the combo box using the form wizard.

1. Open the **Computer Store** database

2. Open the **Products Form** in **Design View**

3. Enlarge the **Detail** section of the report by clicking and dragging the separator labelled **Detail**

4. On the **Form Design** tab in the **Controls** group, click on the **More** downward-facing arrow and select the **Combo Box button**

5. Place the cursor below the **Product Value** text box and click and drag to create the **Combo Box**

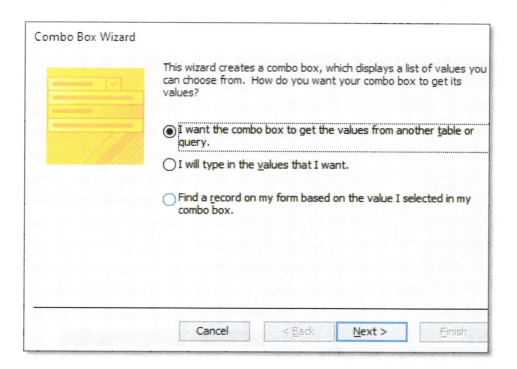

6. The **Combo Box Wizard** appears

7. Select the first option, **I want the combo box to get the values from another table or query**

8. Click **Next**

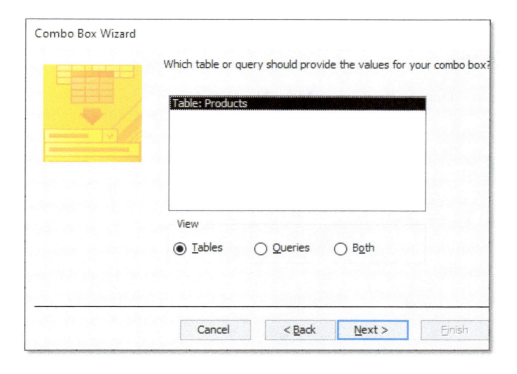

9. Select the **Products** table and select **Tables** under the **View** label

10. Click **Next**

11. Select the **Product** field for the combo box

12. Click on the **Right-hand facing arrow** to select the field

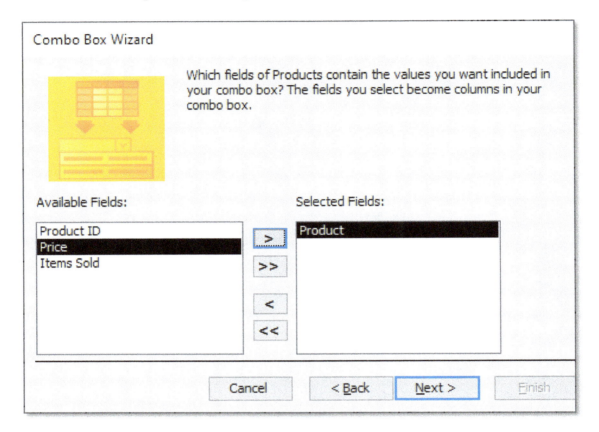

13. Click **Next**

14. Choose to sort the **Products** in **Ascending Order**

15. Click **Next**

16. Accept the list of **Product** names included

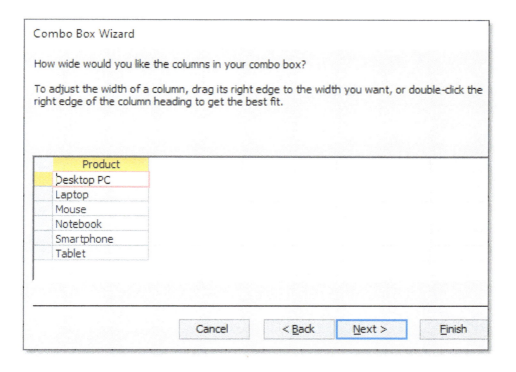

17. Click **Next**

18. Choose to **Remember the value for later use**

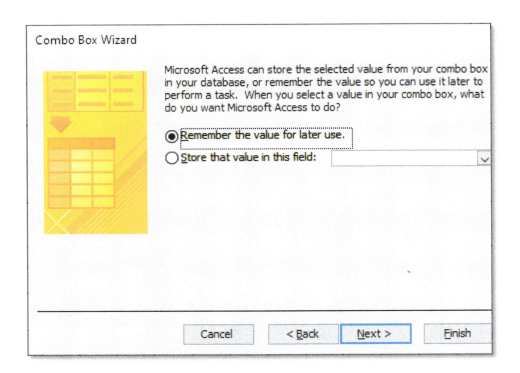

19. Click **Next**

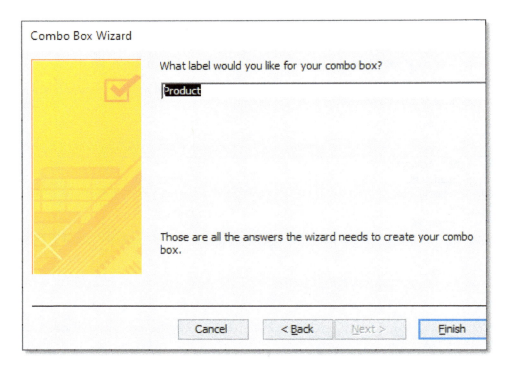

20. Name the label for the combo box as **Product** and click **Finish**

21. Return to **Design View** and rearrange the label and combo box to align with the text boxes above

22. Switch to **Form View** to display the **Combo Box**

23. Save the form and leave it open

Limit to List

In a combo box, it is possible to type in a new value for the set list. It means that only the values already included in the list may be selected using the drop-down list.

1. Open the **Products Form** in **Design View**

2. Display the **Property Sheet** for the **Product** combo box

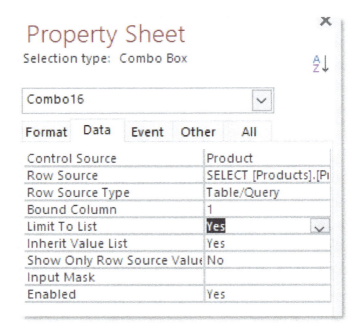

3. On the **Data** tab, click on the **Limit to List** drop-down arrow and select **Yes**

4. This setting will ensure that only entries contained within the combo box list will be displayed

5. Display the form in **Form View**

6. Notice how the drop-down list only contains the entries provided

7. Return to the **Form Design** view

8. On the **Data** tab, click on the **Limit to List** drop-down arrow and select **No**

9. Changing this setting will allow you to enter additional entries for the combo box in the **Products** table

10. Display the form in **Form View**

11. Highlight the entry in the **Combo Box**

12. Type in **Computer** and press the **Enter** key

13. You can enter distinct values and values from a predefined list

14. Save the form and leave it open

List Box

A list box is similar to a combo box, except the values for the list can be chosen using up and down arrows. Manual entry is not allowed in a list box. The number of values that appear in the list box depends on the size of the list box created. If the list box is too small, scroll bars will appear, allowing you to scroll through the list of options. For example, in an online car tax form, a user may want to choose the tax band that applies to their car using up and down arrows to select the vehicle's value range.

1. Open the **Products Form** in **Design View**

2. Click on the **More** drop-down arrow and ensure that **Use Control Wizards** is active

3. Select the **List Box** button and click below the combo box. The **List Box Wizard** starts

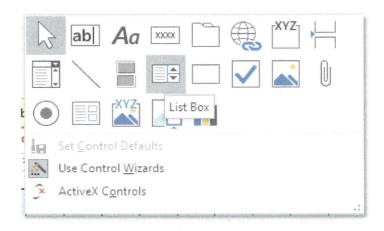

4. Click on the **I will type in the values that I want** option

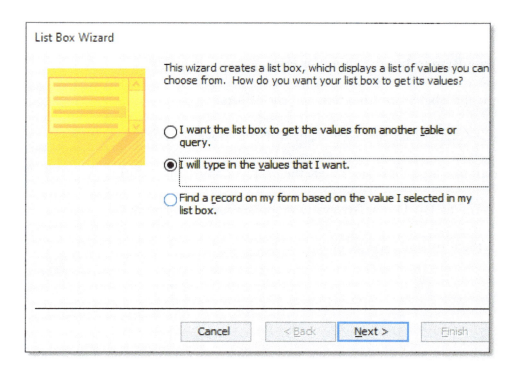

5. Click **Next**

6. Choose a value for the **Number of Columns** as **1**

7. Type in **Glenview, Parkside, Riverfront and Cityview**

8. Press the **Tab** key following each entry to move on to the next

9. Click **Next**

10. Choose **Remember the value for later use** and click **Next**

11. Name the label **Store Location** and click **Finish**

12. Reposition the **List Box** so it aligns with the above labels

13. Return to **Form View** and notice the list box control on the form

14. Click on the **Up-Down Arrows** to move through each option

15. Save the form and leave it open

Check Boxes

Checkboxes are added to forms to allow the user to select a Yes/No type of answer. The user selects a check box if the answer is yes and does not select it when the answer to the question is no. For instance, when a website asks customers whether they would like to subscribe to a newsletter, a checkbox is used to give the customer the option of agreeing to receive a newsletter or not.

1. Open the **Products Form** in **Design View**

2. Enlarge the **Detail** area if required

3. In the **Controls** group, click on the **More** drop-down arrow and select the **Check Box** button

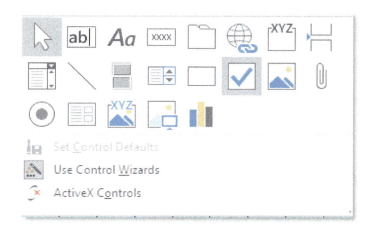

4. Click on the area below the Store Location List Box, and a **Check Box** will appear

5. View the **Property Sheet** for the checkbox

6. On the **Data** tab, select the **Control Source** as **Product**

7. Name the **Label** as **Product Sold**

8. View the form in **Form View**

9. The checkbox will appear on the form

10. Click on the checkbox to select it

11. Advance to the next record

12. Click on the checkbox to deselect it

13. Save the form and leave it open

Option Groups

Option groups enable the user to choose from a list of options on a form. This form element appears as radial buttons on the form. It is a helpful feature that allows you to show all options within a group and allows the user to choose one option from that group. For example, option groups show when asking a customer whether they are male or female.

1. Open the **Products Form** in **Design View**

2. Make sure the **Use Control Wizards** option is active

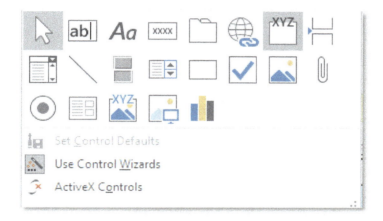

3. Click on the **Option Group** button

4. Click on the area of the form below the **Check Box**

5. The **Option Group Wizard** appears

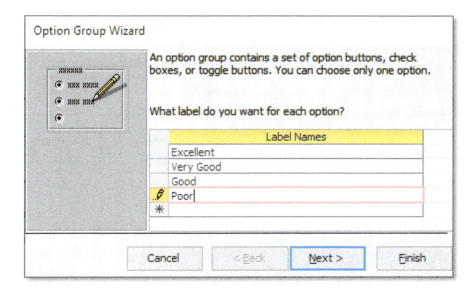

6. For **Label Names** type in **Excellent, Very Good, Good & Poor**

7. Press the **Tab** key to move on to the next entry

8. Click **Next**

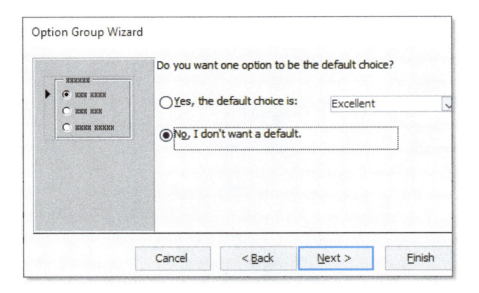

9. Chose **No, I don't want a default**

10. Click **Next**

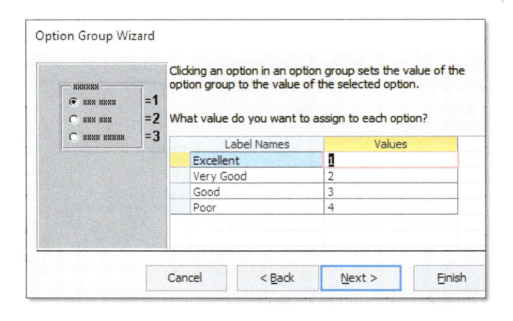

11. Accept the default settings and click **Next**

12. Choose to **Save the values for later use** and click **Next**

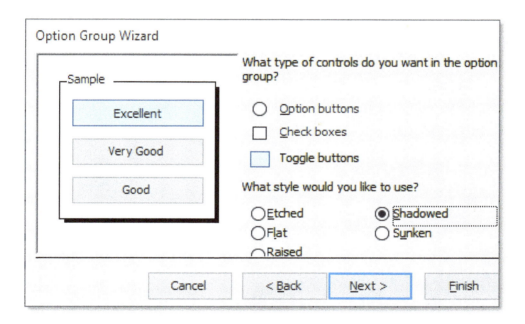

13. For the type of controls in the option group, select **Toggle Buttons**

14. Choose a style of **Shadowed**

15. Click **Next**

16. Name the label as **Service** and click **Finish**

17. Position the label to the left of the **Option Group**

18. Switch to **Form View** and test out the **Option Group**

19. Advance through each record and evaluate the **Service** with different options by clicking on the **Toggle Buttons**

20. Save the form and leave it open

Form Tabs

You may adjust the order of form elements in design view without using the wizard. It gives you greater control over how the form will appear. For example, a manager may show sales for each department with above average figures.

1. Open the **Products Report** in **Design View**

2. On the **Form Design** tab in the **Tools** group, select **Tab Order**

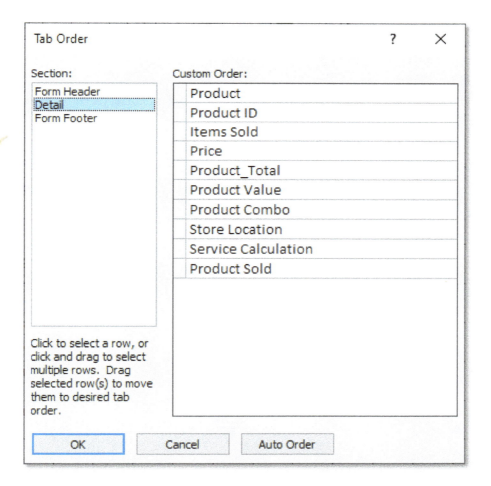

3. Rename each **Text Box** to match the above values

4. You can achieve this by entering in values on the **Property Sheet** tab on the **Other** tab in the **Name** Property

5. Highlight the **Product Sold** tab

6. Click and drag it to position it below **Items Sold**

7. Rearrange the other tabs so they appear as the list above

8. Click and drag to highlight the **Product Total, Product Value** and **Product Combo** tabs

9. Drag and drop the tabs beneath **Product**

10. Click on the **Auto Order** button

11. It arranges tabs automatically

12. Save the form and leave it open

Creating Subforms

A subform is a smaller form within a form created without using a wizard. With the control wizard turned off in design view, you click on the subform/subreport button.

For example, a database may contain information about each customer stored in a car manufacturer's database. A form displays customer information, and a subform shows the details of cars purchased. It allows you to view customer details and information about the vehicle they own.

1. Open the **Products Form** in **Design View**

2. On the **Form Design** tab in the **Controls** group, select **Subform/Subreport**

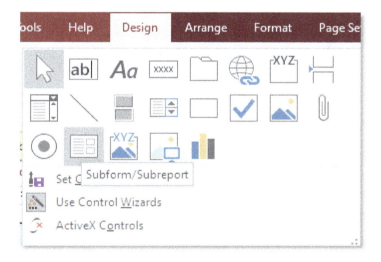

3. Click in a blank space below the **Service** option group

4. The **Subform Wizard** will appear

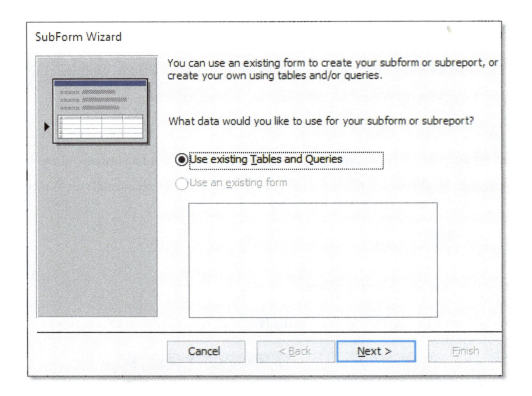

5. Choose **Use Existing Tables and Queries**

6. Select **Next**

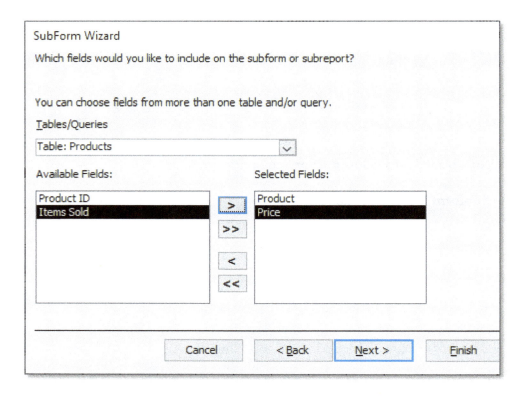

7. Choose the **Products Table** to include in the **Subform**

8. Select **Product** and **Price** fields by clicking the **Right-hand facing arrow**

9. Click **Next**

10. Select **Choose from a list** and select the **Show Products for each Record in Products using Price**

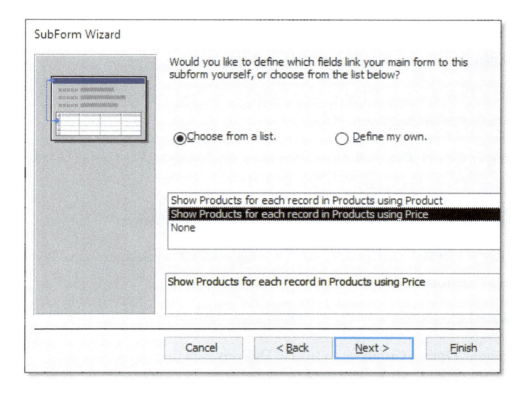

11. Click **Next**

12. Name the subform **Products Subform** and click **Finish**

13. It creates the subform

14. On the **Design** tab, click the **Property Sheet** button in the **Tools** group

15. Click on the **Data** tab and ensure that the **Source Object** is from **Products.Subform**

16. Switch to **Form View** and notice the subform placed in the form

17. Move on to the next slide and notice the change in the **Subform**

18. Select the **Reports.Products** subreport and **Delete** it

19. Save the form and close it

Revision Section 4

1. Open the database **PC Sales**

2. Create a **Text Box** that calculates the **Total Amount Sold** for each product using an expression that multiplies the **Price** by the number of **Items Sold**

3. Format the calculation in **Euros** to **Zero** decimal places

4. Add a **Text Box** that displays "High Value" if the **Price** is over €20 and "Low Value" if it is under €20 labelled **Value**

5. Create a **Combo Box** to display the following list: Excellent, Very Good, Good, Poor, with a label of **Service Quality**

6. **Limit the list** of the **Combo Box** to the entries already entered

7. Create a **List Box** that includes the following entries: Highfield, Cityview, Riverside, with a label of **Store Location**

8. Create a **Check Box** with a label of **Guaranteed** linked to the **Sales** table

9. Create an **Option Group** with a label of **Delivery** with the entries: In Store, Online Pickup, Online

10. Reorder the form tabs so **Items Sold** appears below **Price**

11. Create a **Subform** that includes **Product** and **Price** from the **Source Object Sales** table

12. Save the form as **Sales Form** and close the database

Summary

Forms

In this section, you have learned:

- Form creation using text boxes, combo boxes, and radial buttons

- Subforms and how to embed them in main forms

- Formatting, control sources and values in forms

Section 5

Reports

In this section, you will learn how to:

- Create, modify and design reports

- Include calculated fields such as cumulative sums

- Embed subreports in main reports

Calculated Controls

Calculated fields in a report show percentages and display currency. These fields can display the value of each detail line as a percentage of the report total. You can apply currency formatting to financial fields. It is useful when you want to show formatting relevant to your report.

For example, in a financial report for an organisation, sales figures can be represented by percentages of the annual revenue. Currency formatting can be applied to display sales totals in a chosen currency.

1. Open the **Digital Skills Courses** database

2. Open the **Courses** report

3. View the report in **Design View**

4. On the **Report Design** tab, click on **Group & Sort**

5. At the bottom of the window, notice that the form is grouped by **College** and sorted by **Course**

6. Choose to group by **Location**

7. Then **Sort** by **College**

8. Then **Sort** by **Price** from **Largest to Smallest**

9. View the form in **Form View**

10. Enlarge the **Report Footer**

11. In the **Controls** group, click on **Text Box**

12. Create the **Text Box** beneath the **Page Number** text box

13. Type in the following calculation:

    =sum([Price])

14. Change the label to read **Total Price**

15. On the **Property Sheet** pane, change the format of the **Total Price** text box to **Euro**

16. Change the number of decimal places to **One** for the **Total Price** text box

17. Create another textbox beneath the **Total Price** text box

18. Type in the following calculation:

    =count([Course])

19. Give the text box a label of **No. of Courses**

20. Align the **Total Price** and **Report View** text boxes

21. Return to **Report View**

22. Notice the calculations in the **Report Footer**

23. Return to **Design View** and create another **Text Box** beneath the **No. of Courses** calculation

24. Type in the following calculation:

    =Avg([Price])

25. It will find the average price of courses provided

26. Apply a **Euro** currency to the average course price with **No Decimal Places**

27. Label the text box **Average Course Price**

28. Return to **Report View**

29. Notice the calculations at the bottom of the report

30. Save the form and leave it open

Running Sums

A series of running sums show values that increase as each value within the report appears. For example, this can calculate cumulative sales for each staff member in a department or organisation. The total will add the calculated sales for employees and display it as the department total.

1. Open the **Digital Skills Courses** database

2. On the **Create** tab, locate the **Reports** group and select **Report Wizard**

3. Create a **Report** based on the **Courses** table

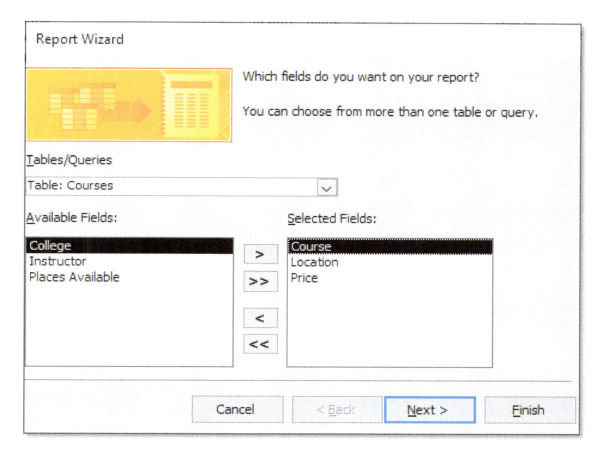

4. Include the **Course, Location & Price** fields

5. Click **Next**

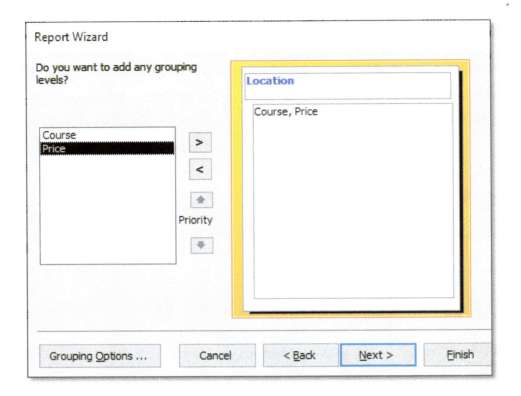

6. Select the **Grouping Level** as **Location**

7. Click on the **Right-hand facing arrow**

8. It will group the report by **Location**

9. Click **Next**

10. Order the **Course** group in **Ascending Order**

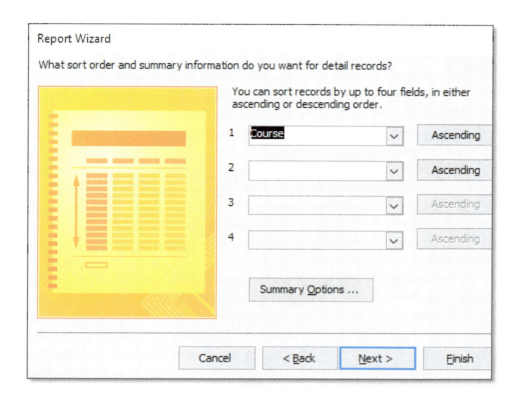

11. Click on **Summary Options**

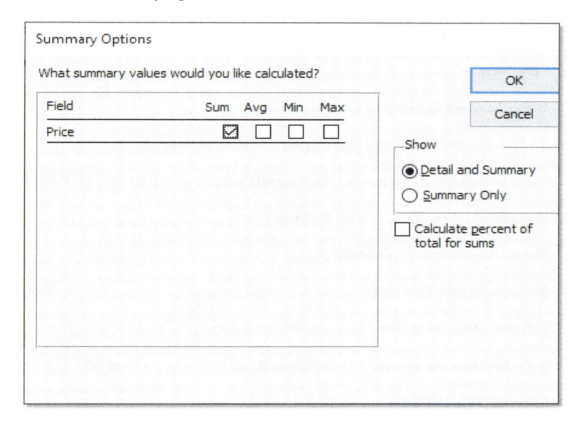

12. Select the **Sum** checkbox

13. Click **OK**

14. Click **Next**

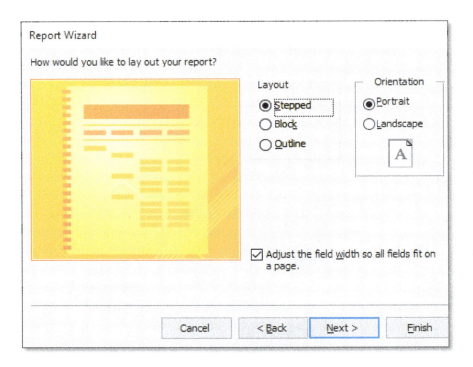

15. Leave the **Layout** as **Stepped** and **Orientation** as **Portrait**

16. Click **Next**

17. Name the report **Course Prices** and click **Finish**

18. To make the **Price Sum** field a running total, switch to **Design View**

19. View the **Property Sheet** pane for the **=sum([Price])** field in the **Location Footer**

20. Select the **Data** tab and search for **Running Sum**

21. Change the setting to **Over Group**

22. Return to **Report View** and notice how the total price for each location is cumulative

23. Return to **Design View** and display the **Property Sheet** pane for the **=sum([Price])** field

24. Select the **Data** tab and for **Running Sum,** change the setting to **Over All**

25. Return to **Report View**

26. The group totals are now cumulative over the entire report

27. Save the report and leave it open

Concatenate Fields

A concatenate calculation links text from two fields together into a single field. You can add text fields together to produce a text string, e.g. a first name added to a surname in a calculated field will produce a full name in the concatenated field.

1. Open the **Students** report

2. Notice the separate **First Name** and **Surname** fields

3. Switch to **Design View**

4. To create a field that includes both the **First Name** and the **Surname**, we will have to use a **Concatenate** calculation

5. Adjust the width of both the **First Name** and the **Surname** fields

6. Add a **Label** with the text **Full Name** to the **Page Header**

7. Include a **Text Box** after both fields in the **Detail** area containing the following formula:

   =[First Name] & " " & [Surname]

8. It will combine both the **First Name** and **Surname** fields

9. View the report in **Report View**

10. Notice how the fields combine to create a text field with each student's full name

11. Save the report and leave it open

Headers & Footers

Data fields can be added to headers and footers in a report to display information, e.g. to include the date and time. Group headers and footers appear within group levels in the design view. Report headers and footers appear at the beginning and end of each report. Page headers at the top of each page and footers at the bottom of each printed page.

1. Open the **Courses** report

2. Switch to **Design View**. Enlarge the **Report Footer** and create a **Text Box**

3. Label the **Text Box** as **Total Price** and type in the following calculation:

   =Sum([Price])

4. Format the calculation in **Euro** currency with **No Decimal Places**

5. Return to **Form View**

6. Notice that the calculation appears at the bottom of the report

7. In the **Page Header** draw a **Text Box**

8. Delete the **Label**. Enter the following formula into the **Text Box:**

   =Now()

9. This calculation will display the current date & time

10. Return to **Report View** and notice that the current date and time appear in the header

11. Right-click on the current date and time in the report header and select **Cut**

12. Right-click in the **Group Footer** and choose **Paste**

13. Return to **Report View**

14. The current date and time move to the **Group Footer**

15. On the **Property Sheet** pane, change the format to **Long Date**

16. Save the report and close it

Sort Records

Records in a report can be grouped and sorted by fields. Records group together and appear in ascending alphabetical order or descending alphabetical order. For example, apply the group and sort feature to sort employee names in ascending alphabetical order.

1. Open the **Courses** report

2. In the **Grouping & Totals** group, select **Group & Sort**

3. Group the report by **Location with Z on Top**

4. Click on **More** and select the setting **Keep Whole Group Together on One Page**

Group, Sort, and Total

Group on **Location** ▼ with Z on top ▼ , More ▶

Sort by **Course**

Sort by **College**

Add a group   Add a sort

5. Then sort by **Course with A on Top**

6. Then sort by **College with A on Top**

7. Return to **Design View** and notice how the grouping has changed. The order within those groups adjusts according to the settings applied

8. Save the report and leave it open

Page Breaks

Page breaks organise the fields in a report. It forces the fields to appear on a new page and display the data in a structured manner. For example, in a staff report, page breaks make the next employee's details appear on the following page.

1. Open the **Courses** report

2. Switch to **Design View**

3. Double click on the bar across the top of the **Location Header** to show the **Property Sheet** for this section

4. Select the **Format** tab and set the **Force New Page** property to **Before Section** so that each group will start on a new page

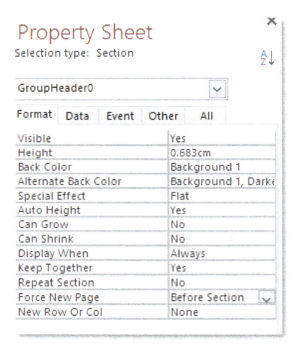

5. Preview the report in **Report View**. Notice how each group is on a new page, and the number of pages has increased.

6. Save the report and leave it open

Subreports

Subreports containing linked information appear within the main report. It is similar to a subform contained within the main form. You can include a subreport in the main report using the subreport wizard. There are several steps to complete to create the subreport.

For example, in a staff list of course instructors, you can place a subreport in the main report showing course details each instructor teaches. Users of the report can then view the courses taught by each instructor.

1. Open the **Courses Report**

2. Switch to **Design View** and enlarge the **Detail** area

3. In the **Controls** group, click on **Subform/Subreport**

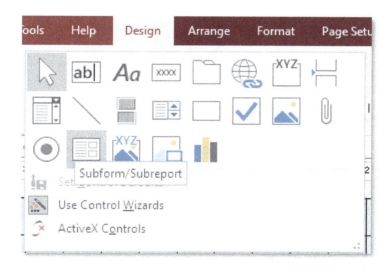

4. Select **Use an Existing Report or Form** and select the **Students** table

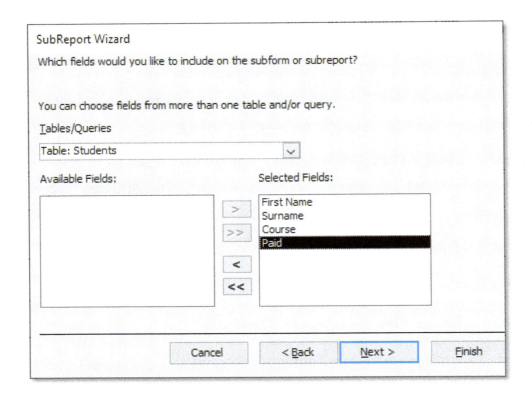

5. Include all **Available Fields** as the **Selected** fields

6. Click **Next**

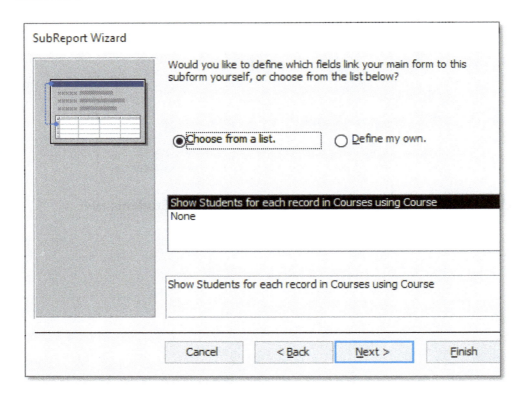

7. Select **Choose from a List** and select **Show Students for each record in Courses** using **Course**

8. Click **Next**

9. Name the Subreport **Students Subreport** and click **Finish**

10. Ensure the **Source Object** is from **Table.Students**

11. The subreport appears in the **Students Report**

12. Close the report

13. Select the **Students Report** and **Delete** it

14. Close the database

Revision Section 5

1. Open the **Digital Skills Courses** database

2. Open the **Courses** report in **Design View**

3. Include a **Text Box** in the **Report Footer** that will find the average price of courses and label it **Average Price**

4. Make the average price calculation a **Running Sum** so that the **average price** for each **College** is cumulative

5. Use a **Concatenate Field** to combine the **College** field with the **Location** field in the **Detail** area and name it **College Location**

6. Move the **Count** calculation field to the **Report Footer** to count all the courses on offer naming it **No. of Courses**

7. Include a **Date & Time** field in the **Report Header** to display the current date and time and delete the accompanying **Label**

8. Sort the records so that details are grouped by **Location** and **Keep the Whole Group Together on One Page**

9. Apply a setting that forces a new page after each **Location Header** section

10. Create a **Subreport** using an existing **Students** table and choose from a list that shows students for each record in courses using **Course**

11. Save the report and close it

Summary

Reports

In this section, you have learned:

- Tab order elements in report design

- Calculations including cumulative sums, count and average

- Subreports and embedding them in main reports

Section 6

Enhancing Productivity

In this section, you will learn how to:

- Import external data from spreadsheets and text files

- Automate tasks using macros

- Build custom macros for specific tasks

Linking External Data

Linking involves creating a table from an external source such as a spreadsheet. Changes to the external source appear in the linked table. For example, you can create a spreadsheet containing budget information linked to a financial report in a database.

1. Open the **Computer Store** database

2. Open the **Products** table

3. On the **External Data** tab, click the **New Data Source** button in the **Import & Link** group

4. Select **From Database** and choose **Access**

5. Click **Browse** and navigate to the **Work Files** folder

6. Select the **PC Sales** database and click **OK**

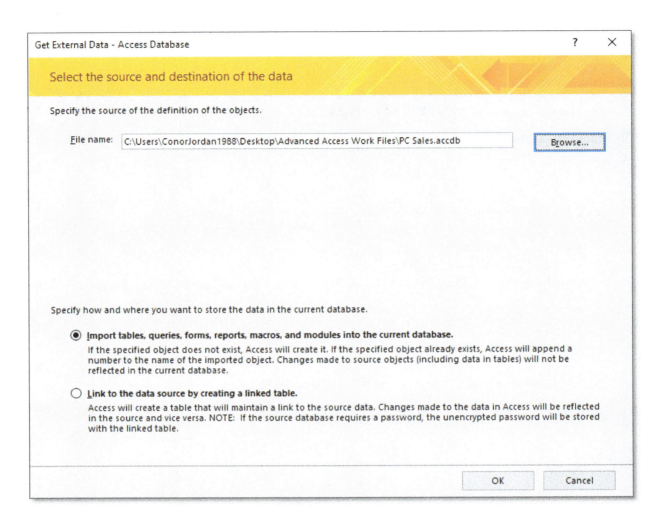

7. Choose **Import tables, queries, forms, reports, macros, and modules into the current database**

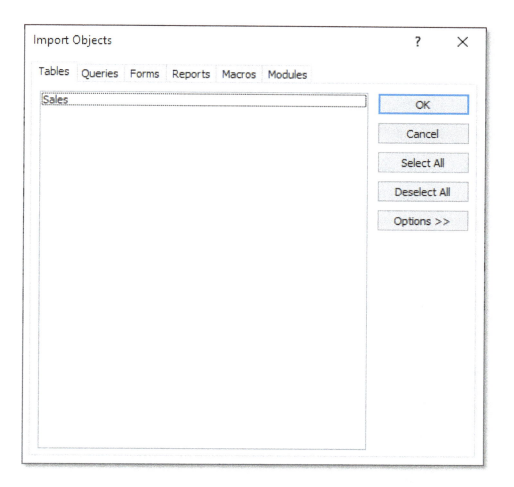

8. Select the **Sales** table and click **OK**

9. Click **Close**

10. The **Sales** table appears in the database

11. Close the database

Importing Spreadsheets

You can import Excel spreadsheets into a database. Importing converts the source data format and creates a new copy within Access. The information is edited in Access and does not change the source file as it is unlinked.

For example, a manager may want to import a spreadsheet containing staff salaries for each department into a monthly database report. The details of employees may not change for that month but may need adjustments in future.

1. Open the **Car Sales** database

2. Open the **Vehicles** table

3. In the **Import & Link** group, choose the option **New Data Source**

4. Choose **From File** and select **Excel**

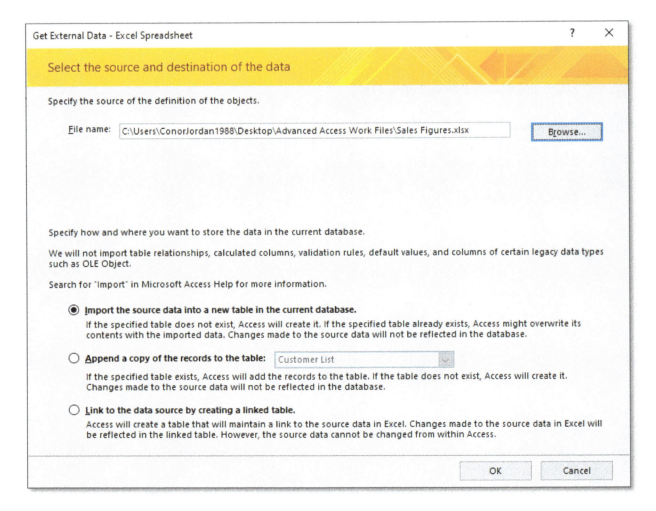

5. Click **Browse** and navigate towards the work files folder

6. Select the **Sales Figures** spreadsheet

7. From the options available, select the **Import the source data into a new table in the current database** radial button

8. Click **OK**

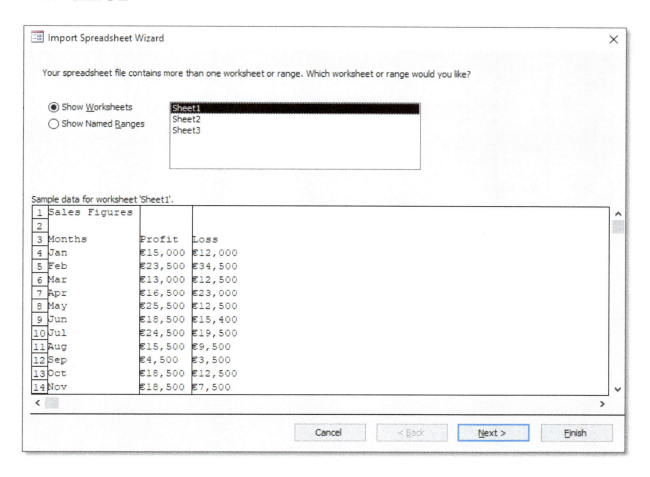

9. Accept the default settings and click **Next**

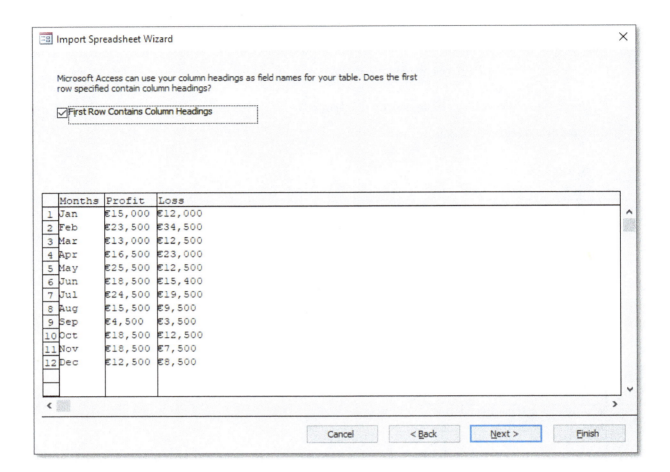

10. Choose the **First Row Contains Column Headings** option

11. Click **Next**

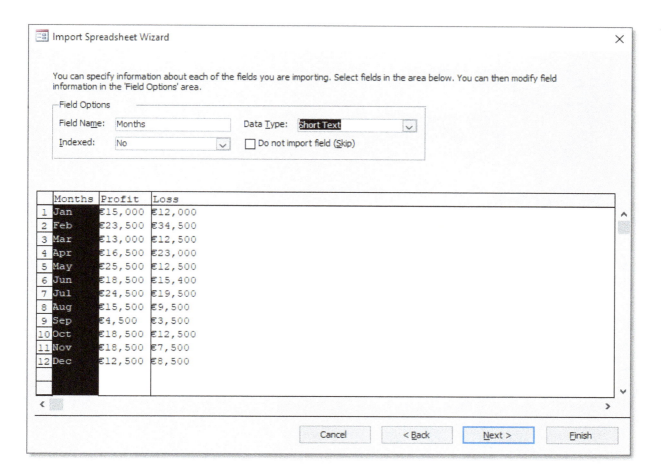

12. Accept the default settings and click on **Next**

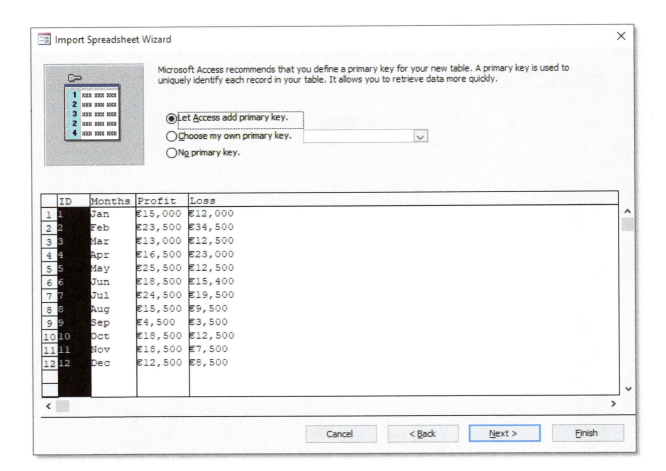

13. Select the option **Let Access add primary key**

14. Click **Finish**

15. Rename the table **Sales Figures**

16. It imports information from the spreadsheet

17. Save and close the database

Importing Text Files

Text files such as a basic text format (.txt) or comma separated variables (.csv) can be imported into a database. The changes made to imported text files do not change the source file. For example, you may want to add a staff list contained within a basic text format file into a database. It imports the text file into the active database.

1. Open the **Car Sales** database and open the **Vehicles** table

2. In the **Import & Link** group, click on **New Data Source**

3. Choose **From File** and select **Text File**

4. Click **Browse** and navigate towards the work files folder

5. Select the **Customer List** text file

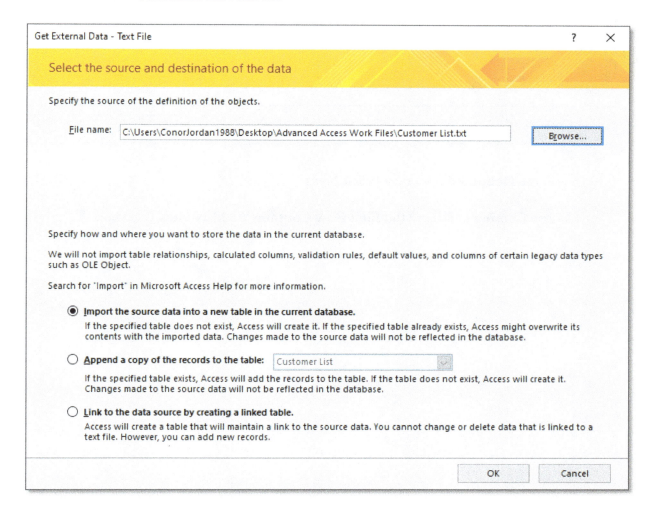

6. Choose the option **Import the Source Data into a new table in the current database**

7. Click **OK**

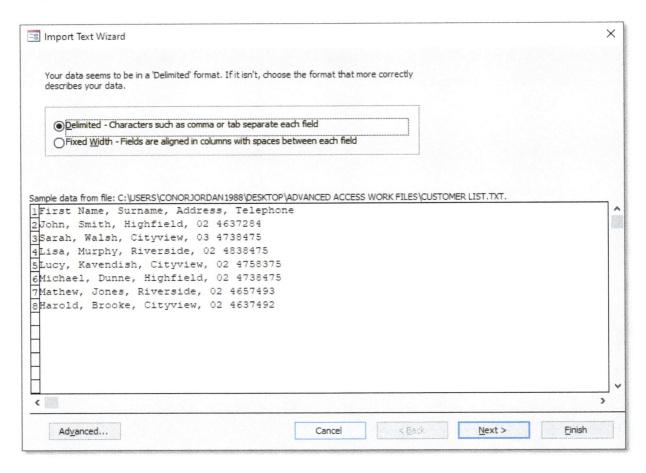

8. Select the **Delimited** option and click **Next**

9. Choose **Comma** and select the **First Row Contains Field Names** checkbox

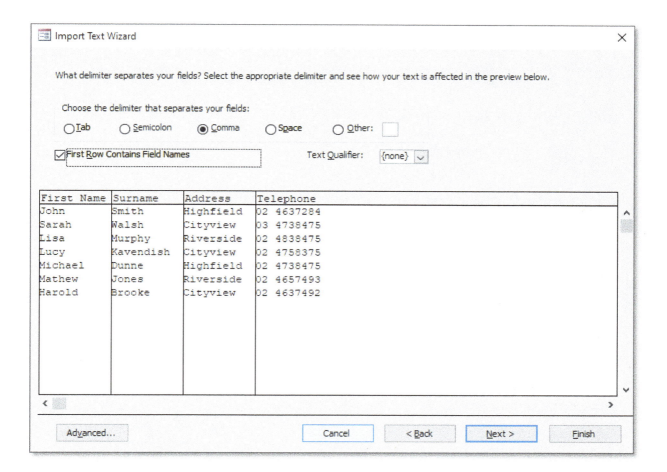

10. Click **Next.** Click **Next** again

11. Select **Let Access Add Primary Key**

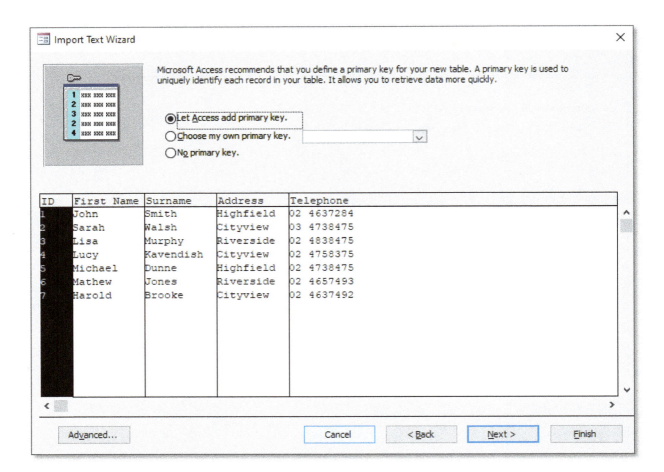

12. Name the table **Customer Details**

13. Click **Finish**

14. Click **Close**

15. The text file will be imported into the database

16. Close the database

Create a Macro

Macros make repetitive tasks in Access easier to complete. Macros record step-by-step tasks as they occur. When the macro runs again, the sequence of recorded tasks runs automatically.

For example, in a report with calculated fields, percentages and currency calculations can be created automatically using a macro to save time for the database user. A macro can automatically print and close a report.

1. Open the **Digital Skills Courses** database

2. On the **Create** tab, locate the **Macros & Code** group, select **Macro**

3. From the drop-down list, choose **OpenReport**

4. Select **Add New Action**

5. From the drop-down list, select **MinimiseWindow**

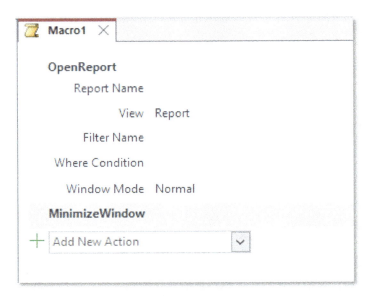

6. Save the macro as **OpenCourses** by right-clicking on the **Macro** tab

7. Leave the database open

Attaching a Macro to a Control

A macro can be attached to different controls such as an image, command button or a data field. The macro runs when you click on the image, button, or data field. An event needs to be set up in the control's properties to tell the macro when to carry out its tasks, e.g. on a single click of the mouse or a double click of the mouse.

1. In the **Digital Skills Courses** database, create a new macro.

2. Set the **Command** as **PrintObject** and save the macro as **Print**

3. Open the **Courses** report by double-clicking on the **OpenCourses** macro

4. Display the form in **Design View**

5. Ensure that the **Use Control Wizards** button is inactive

6. Create a **Command Button** in the **Report Footer**

7. View its **Property Sheet** and select the **Event** tab

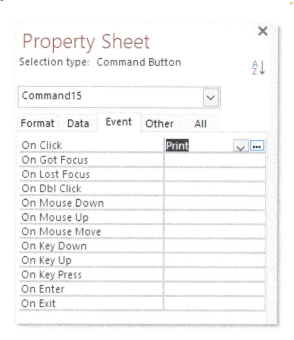

8. Select the drop-down arrow for **On Click** and choose **Print**

9. Rename the button, **Print**

10. Switch to **Report View** and click the button in the Report. The macro is run and will print the report

11. Save the database and leave it open

Attaching a Macro to an Object

Macros can make carrying out repetitive tasks more efficient. Macros can be attached to a database object, form, or report. You may set up a macro to run when a report opens, saves, and closes.

1. Open the **Digital Skills Courses** database

2. Open the **Courses** report in **Design View**

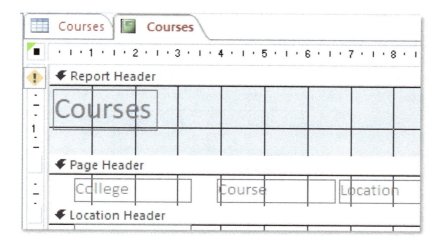

3. Click on the button in the top left to select the entire form

4. Display the **Property Sheet** and select the **Event tab**

5. Click in **On Close** and select the **Print** macro. It will print the report every time the report is closed

6. Switch to **Form View** and close the **Report**

7. The **Print** dialog box appears, prompting you to print the report

8. Save and close the report leaving the database open

Attaching a Macro to a Button

Macros can be added to command buttons using a wizard. When you click on the button, the macro will run. For instance, when you review a report, a macro runs to save and print the report when you click a button with an attached macro.

1. In the **Digital Skills Courses** database, open the **Courses** report

2. Open the report in **Design View** and ensure that **Use Control Wizards** is active

3. Create a **Command Button** in the **Report Footer**

4. Right-click on the **Command Button** and choose **Build Event**

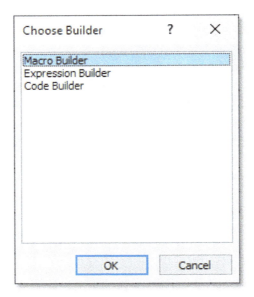

5. Choose the **Macro Builder** and click **OK**

6. Select the **CloseWindow Macro** with an **Object Type** as **Report**

7. Set the **Object Name** as **Courses,** and for **Save,** select **Yes**

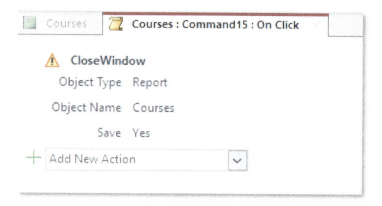

8. Select a **SaveRecord** action after the **CloseWindow** action

9. Save the macro as **Save and Close**

10. Return to **Design View** and on the **Property Sheet** on the **Event** tab, select **OnClick** and choose the **Save and Close** macro

11. Return to the **Report View** and click on the macro

12. The report will be saved and closed

13. Save the database and close it

Revision Section 6

1. Open the **Orders** database

2. Import the **Products** table from the **Computer Store** database

3. Import the **Staff List** spreadsheet into the **Orders** database

4. Allow Access to add a **Primary Key** to the imported information

5. Import the **Customer List** text file into a new table in the **Orders** database and choose a delimited option of commas

6. Create an **OpenTable** macro for the **Customers** table in **Read Only** mode called **Customers Open**

7. With the **Report Wizard,** create a **Report** using the information from the **Customers** table

8. Create a **Command Button** that will print the report each time it is closed

9. Create another macro that **Saves** the report when it is closed

10. Click on the **Command Button** and notice the effect

11. Close the **Report** and notice the saved changes

12. Save the database and close it

Summary

Database Concepts

In this section, you have learned:

- Getting data from external sources such as CSV files

- Applying macros to repetitive tasks such as automatic printing

- Creating custom macro buttons for auto-saving

Index

www.ingramcontent.com/pod-product-compliance
Lightning Source LLC
Chambersburg PA
CBHW081228050326
40690CB00014B/2696